CLASS

MATTERS

CLASS
MATTERS

CORRESPONDENTS OF
The New York Times

INTRODUCTION BY
BILL KELLER

TIMES BOOKS
HENRY HOLT AND COMPANY, NEW YORK

Times Books
Henry Holt and Company, LLC
Publishers since 1866
175 Fifth Avenue
New York, New York 10010
www.henryholt.com

Library of Congress Cataloging-in-Publication Data

Class matters / correspondents of the New York Times ; introduction by Bill Keller.
        p. cm.
    Collected from a series of articles published in the New York Times in the
spring of 2005.
    ISBN-13: 978-0-8050-8055-1
    ISBN-10: 0-8050-8055-4
    1. Social classes—United States. 2. Social mobility—United States. 3 Social
values—United States. 4. Social stratification—United States. 5. Social classes—
United States—Case studies. I. New York times.

HN90.S6C565 2005
305.5'13'0973—dc22

                                                                    2005050686

First Edition 2005

Designed by Meryl Sussman Levavi
Illustrations edited by Macaulay Campbell

Printed in the United States of America
20   19   18   17   16   15   14   13   12

Contents

Introduction

BILL KELLER

I guess it's safe to admit now that at its genesis and at several points along the way this whole undertaking seemed potentially an act of folly. *The New York Times* has a history of deploying teams of talented people for long periods on big, hard subjects. In 2000 we had taken on the subject of race, not as a political construct or an exercise in demography but more intimately, as a force in how we live our lives. In 1993, we had invested an immense effort in illuminating how poverty twists the lives of children. In each case it felt as if we had reinvented what a newspaper series could be. But from the first stirrings of this project in the late summer of 2003 it was clear that the subject of class was more formidable—vast, amorphous, politically charged, largely unacknowledged. In a country where the overwhelming majority of people identify themselves in polls as "middle class," there seemed to be no consensus as to what class meant, let alone whether it mattered.

That the idea was not abandoned at the outset has much to do with an extraordinary editor, Soma Golden Behr, who had presided over both of those earlier projects—"How Race Is Lived in America" and "Children of the Shadows." Soma is not easily intimidated, either by riptides of data (she began as an economics reporter) or by the sneers of conventional wisdom. She is tenacious in her passions but voraciously open to contrary argument. She is notoriously deliberative, and yet, when you're about to tear your hair out because the meeting has gone on an hour too long or the project is a month overdue, she delivers, and what she delivers is original and excellent.

This project was conceived one hot weekend in the Berkshires, where Soma was visiting an old friend, a University of Pennsylvania sociologist named Frank Furstenberg. Soma was yearning aloud for one more Big Thing as she approached mandatory retirement. Furstenberg, an expert on how urban poverty affects families, told her that the *Times* should think of "doing class." Soma initially recoiled. What could you say about class beyond the obvious pieties—the widening income gap, the slow demise of the blue-collar middle, the struggle of the underclass—all worthy subjects but amply documented in our pages and elsewhere? Was there something new enough to justify a big commitment of reporting time and reader attention?

When Soma first approached me with the idea it was still just an intriguing notion. We began assembling groups of reporters and editors from different sections of the paper for brainstorming sessions that were long, intense, and inconclusive. What *is* class, after all? Is it just about money? Education? Social status? There was deep disagreement between those who thought class was the governing force in American life and those who deemed it pretty much irrelevant. (The argument would never be entirely resolved. For much of the year that followed, at least one member of the reporting team insisted that this was a big waste of time—even as she worked on and finally delivered one of the most engaging chapters of the series.) Soma enlisted two agile and contrarian editing minds early on—Tom Kuntz, who would remain her hands-on sidekick throughout the series, and Jon Landman, an early believer in the project who would serve as a kind of kibitzer-in-chief.

And then we did what we do: we reported. Soon after Thanksgiving, we deployed two reporters to go prospecting. David Leonhardt, an economics reporter with a show-me turn of mind, had already become fascinated by new research questioning the American assumptions about mobility—how readily people move up or down the ladder of prosperity and status. Janny Scott, a reporter with an unusual gift for rendering complicated subjects accessible, dug into new thinking about the impact of class on health, immigration, residential segregation, and child rearing. They spent the next few months grilling economists, sociologists, and marketing experts, wrangling data. Their inquiries were interrupted by breaking news stories, including a presidential election campaign, and by the birth of David's son, but by the spring they reported back that, yes, there was much new and surprising to be said about class.

"It was beginning to become clear to most economists that mobility in the United States was neither what they had long believed nor what most Americans took for granted," Janny said. "Also, class had become more, not less, of a predictor of who was getting into elite four-year colleges. Class differences in health and lifespan appeared not to be shrinking but widening. Class seemed to be playing an increasingly, rather than decreasingly, powerful role in where Americans were choosing to live: analyses of data from the last three censuses showed that the affluent had become more and more isolated from everyone else. There were other trends, too. It appeared that Americans had become less likely to marry across class lines than they once were, and class differences in family structure and child rearing were on the rise."

At the same time, other factors were making America *appear* less class-bound than ever. The general rise in affluence had obscured the traditional class markers and distorted the old class-based political alignments. It was no longer so easy to guess a person's place in the social hierarchy by his race or religion or possessions.

"It was the contradiction that fascinated us," Janny recalled. "At a time when, by many measures, class seemed less and less a force in American life, it had become more so in some of the areas that matter most."

Identifying these surprising and provocative themes was a breakthrough, but the *Times* is not in the dissertation business. Yes, we like to write about ideas—indeed, for the first piece in this series we decided to have Janny and David lay out our findings in essay form—but it is asking a lot of readers to stick with a (now quite literally) book-length exploration of a complicated subject, especially one that most Americans prefer not to talk about. We needed to animate the trends and test them against real experience, to supply characters and narrative. For journalists bred to the metabolic rate of a daily newspaper, this is tortuous work. It is easy to harvest sound bites, but it is a labor of patience to search out people who embody the trends, to persuade them to admit a reporter into their confidence, and then to pay close attention over the days or weeks or months while the insights emerge.

In early April 2004 we approved the project and liberated a team of reporters from their daily assignments—telling ourselves we hoped to finish the series and return the reporters to their beats before the end of the year but knowing from experience that that was unlikely. The writers then dispersed in search of the stories that would illuminate, sharpen, or possibly contradict, their working hypotheses.

Janny Scott took as her map the newfound statistical evidence showing that the upper middle class lived longer and healthier lives than the middle class, which in turn did better than the working class. The evidence indicated that this was not just about access to health care. It reflected class differences in working conditions, stress, diet, neighborhood, family structure, and a host of other social and economic factors. Early on, she settled on heart attacks—events with a known cause and a quick dramatic arc—as a way of illustrating how illness plays out differently in different classes. It was an excellent idea, but how do you identify a cast of characters who are more or less representative of particular classes, victims of heart attacks in approximately the same time frame, and willing to let a reporter into their lives? Janny spent months courting interventional cardiologists, the doctors who see patients immediately after their heart attacks. At one point she was given a temporary employee ID at a hospital so she could trail along behind a cardiologist from bed to bed as he made his rounds three times a week. Eventually she accumulated dozens of subjects who were willing to have a reporter intrude in their lives, and from this sample she picked three—an architect, a utility worker, and a housekeeper—whose experiences before, during, and after their heart attacks powerfully illustrate that class can be, literally, a matter of life and death.

To a greater or lesser degree, most members of the reporting team performed similar feats of tedious investigation before finding characters who would personify the statistical trends.

Peter Kilborn, a Washington-based business reporter, set out to study what seemed to be a growing geographical isolation by class: subdivisions segregated not by race, religion, or ethnic origin but by increments of income. He pored over census data for places where the incomes were conspicuously stratified, and settled on Alpharetta, Georgia—a town of about 37,000 to which he would bring no preconceptions because he had never heard of it before. Then he made it his home away from home and began painstakingly to learn the town from the ground up, while searching for a family whose experience would carry a narrative. Like many sprawling residential towns, Alpharetta has no central gathering spot. "People are always in their cars, at work or school, or tucked inside the subdivisions where most live," Peter said. So he began making the rounds of garage and moving sales where he would linger and chat, and at those driveway gatherings he kept hearing an unfamiliar word: "relo." The term, "relocation" abbreviated, was used as noun and verb to describe the nomadic lives of white-collar families employed by global companies. The "relos" move periodically from place to place but usually resettle into a neighborhood much like the one they left, adjoined by other subdivisions just a price point richer or poorer. Peter burrowed deep into the lives of four different families before selecting as his window into the "relo" class the family of Jim Link, a financial services sales manager he found serving beer at the opening of a subdivision swimming pool.

Tamar Lewin, who had insinuated herself in the world of teenage girls for a memorable chapter in the race series, knew from the beginning that she wanted to write about class divisions within families. Through a posting on a school librarians' Web site she sought out family reunions, where she imagined she would encounter interesting frictions between prosperous siblings and relatives still mired at the bottom. But after several weekends spent encamped with multiple generations of families, she realized that reunions are "the worst possible place to see class differences," since they are occasions where people go out of their way to suppress what divides them. Next she began seeking out cross-class marriages, which proved a different exercise in journalistic frustration. There the difficulty was getting the couples to talk openly about their class baggage. "The working-class wife would talk freely about their different views of gift giving, vacations, food, child rearing, money," Tamar recalled, "but her upper-middle husband would take exception, saying he thought those differences were a matter of personality, gender, education, religion, geography—*anything* but class." She finally found her subjects—Dan Croteau and Cate Woolner—through a group in western Massachusetts that runs workshops for people in cross-class relationships.

David Leonhardt set out to pursue the role of class in higher education. His research had told him that although quality universities have filled their classrooms with a conspicuous diversity of students, low-income students were dropping out at an astounding rate and graduating classes were even more tilted toward the upper classes than in the past. He knew, too, that the passport to success in America is not getting into college but finishing with a four-year degree. Thus a system idealized as a great equalizer serves to reinforce the advantages of birth. His long search for a way to humanize this profound generalization ended in a coffee shop at the University of Virginia, where David was interviewing Leanna Blevins, a Ph.D. student from a largely poor region in the southwest corner of Virginia, one of those hoisted up by a college degree. Did she happen to have a childhood friend or high school classmate who had taken a different path? he asked. "Oh, you need to meet my brother," she replied.

Each member of our reporting team found fresh insights. Anthony DePalma, a veteran foreign and domestic correspondent, spotted an important twist in the destiny of immigrants, who loom so large in the great American myth. Tony noticed that Mexicans, who make up the fastest growing immigrant population, have been far less successful at moving up from the bottom than many earlier immigrant waves. The reasons for that are complicated, and Tony gave them flesh and blood by befriending some Mexican kitchen workers at a restaurant owned by an earlier, successful immigrant from Greece. Religion writer Laurie Goodstein and David Kirkpatrick, who had been covering conservative interest groups and their constituencies, discovered the little-noticed migration of evangelical Christians from the social margins into the Protestant social mainstream, as illustrated by the growing influence of evangelicals on Ivy League campuses.

On a project this ambitious, even great reporters will drill some dry holes. Our first attempt to explore how consumer product companies exploit class foundered when a major cosmetics company, which initially agreed to let a reporter inside their marketing department, got cold feet. Some lines of reporting were dropped or condensed into sidebars after months of work simply because the material seemed too familiar—the part class plays in determining who goes to war was one, the diminished role of blue-collar manu-facturing as a class escalator was another. Good stories but too often told. We wanted to break new ground.

One patch of new ground that made us particularly proud emerged from David Cay Johnston's obsessive mining of tax records and other government statistics. David discovered a previously unremarked trend—that the most moneyed Americans, those he called the "hyper-rich," were pulling away from the pack, their share of the nation's wealth growing faster than those of other eco-nomic tiers, even families making hundreds of thousands of dollars a year. Moreover, the Bush tax cuts, David demonstrated, will ben-efit the hyper-rich at the expense of the "merely rich."

Working closely with a former business editor, Glenn Kramon, David labored for months to create a financial portrait of the rich-est Americans. His work was so conscientious that the economic model he developed was pronounced reliable by experts at the Treasury Department and in think tanks on *both* the right and the left. No piece in the series provoked more furious discussion.

Isabel Wilkerson performed a different but equally arduous feat of reporting: reconstructing a life. Isabel, a tenacious reporter and mellifluous writer who returned from a long book-writing leave for this project, had composed one of the most powerful chapters in the 1993 "Children of the Shadows" series. She had told the story of Nicholas Whitiker, a ten-year-old Chicago boy drafted into manhood by his family's economic struggle. When we contact-ed her about the class project, she agreed to re-engage with the Whitikers and see what their experience in the ensuing years had to tell us about how someone at the bottom does—or does not—scrabble up to the middle class. For several months Isabel commuted to Chicago from her home in Atlanta and slowly pieced together a consummately human conclusion to the series that is not a simple happy ending but one laced with hope and heroism.

Roughly fifty people contributed in some significant way to this undertaking. *Times* photographers, coordinated by a superb picture editor, Sarah Weissman, were partners from the outset in most of the reporting, and produced portraits integral to the project. Marjorie Connelly and Rich Meislin designed an innovative poll of American attitudes about class. William Lin, a researcher at *The New York Times Magazine*, was enlisted early on to help with fact-checking and data-mapping. The paper's graphics department, especially Archie Tse and Matthew Ericson, devised intriguing ways to visualize the complicated data underlying the series. Anne Leigh, the art director, laid out visually sumptuous pages. Lon Teter arrived in the final month to serve as, in effect, production foreman—getting an immense and complicated body of work checked, formatted, and into the paper on time. The copy editor for the series, our last line of defense against the stupid mistake or infelicitous phrase, was Joe Rogers. Charles Hanger, Benjamin Werschkul, and Geoff McGhee from Nytimes.com transformed the series into an engaging Web experience, including audio slide shows and interactive graphics.

Overseeing it all were some of the finest editors in journalism, who pushed and questioned, sharpened and refined: Soma and Tom Kuntz, of course; Chip McGrath, who also contributed an erudite essay on the evolution of class as a theme in American popular culture; John Darnton; and Bill McDonald.

I take it as a tribute to our foresight that as our work was moving toward print, both *The Wall Street Journal* and the *Los Angeles Times* decided to dig mines in roughly the same terrain we had been excavating for these many months—the *Journal* looking at the difficulty of moving up the socioeconomic ladder, the *L.A. Times* at the perils of falling off it. The reporters and editors on our class team were not sure whether to welcome the company or bemoan the competition (especially as a *Journal* piece touching on some of our conclusions about mobility appeared a few days before the announced launch of our series). When all was published and done, my competitive anxieties, at least, had been allayed. With due respect for the fine work of other papers, I'm confident the reporting represented in these pages takes the discussion of class in our country to a new level.

As it happens, during the year that these stories were in preparation I spent a good deal of time giving speeches and interviews about what seemed to me a worrying decline in the credibility of the news media. Our diminished standing, I argued, is a consequence partly of serial scandals in the news media, partly of the cynicism of a more polarized electorate, and partly of concerted assaults from vociferous partisans, right and left. I believe, though, that the underlying reason for the waning of public trust is the way we have retreated from the hard labor of journalism under grinding commercial pressure, the steady downsizing and dumbing down, the pandering, the substitution of dueling blowhards and celebrity gossip for actual reporting. My prescription, when anyone asked, was more ambitious journalism—launching the best reporters at the hardest subjects, and holding their reporting and thinking to the highest standards. There is no greater antidote to the public cynicism about the press than seeing the labor and thought and scrupulous care that go into producing a masterful piece of journalism. Like this one.

CLASS

MATTERS

ERMA GOULART, SELF-DESCRIBED CLASS: LOWER

Goulart, sixty-seven years old, a widowed retiree with a high school education, strung beads for a jewelry maker, worked for sewage and coal companies, and owned a restaurant. "I worked hard for what I have," she said. She sees unfairness. "The rich get more benefits and tax breaks and the poor people don't," she said. "Being raised poor, it was kind of hard," she recalled. She helped bring up her eleven siblings and now does the same for her disabled sister's children. "I think the American dream is to help people," Goulart said.

MAURICE MITCHELL, SELF-DESCRIBED CLASS: WORKING

Mitchell, thirty-seven years old, manages his family's septic tank company, earning up to $75,000 a year. "I hold the mortgage to my home," he said. "I have the vehicle I want." A high school graduate, he never married but has two sons. "I'm able to raise my children in a manner so they won't be picked on or laughed at in school." He said he believed that "a man can start with nothing and work hard and get somewhere." But the "gap between rich and poor will never close," he said. "It's hard to get wealthy if your family isn't."

STEVE SCHOENECK, SELF-DESCRIBED CLASS: MIDDLE

Schoeneck, thirty-nine years old, is an accounting manager for an electrical utility. He and his wife, a preschool teacher, both college graduates, earn $85,000 a year. They have two daughters in school and a son, a sophomore at MIT. "You always have the opportunity to try and move forward financially," he said. "For me, the American dream is to earn a reasonable living and to be able to spend quality time with my family and my friends in a community that cares. Overall, I've achieved the American dream. I'm happy."

BARBARA FREEBORN, SELF-DESCRIBED CLASS: UPPER

Freeborn, forty-seven years old, a marketing executive, and her husband, a business owner, earn more than $150,000 a year. To her, the rich get "preferential treatment, where they don't have to pay for things." But she sees many opportunities to make money now, "in technology and health care and finance." Still, she said, America has changed since her parents' generation. "I don't think they really aspired to have more than the house with a porch and to come home and have dinner." Today, she said, "everybody wants more."

1. Shadowy Lines That Still Divide

Janny Scott and David Leonhardt

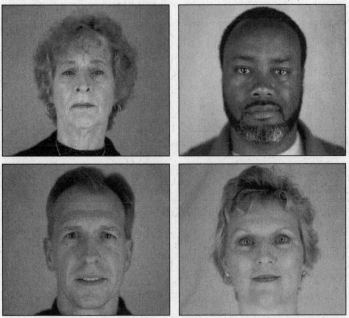

Four faces of social class in America today. Top, Erma Goulart, Maurice Mitchell. Bottom, Steve Schoeneck, Barbara Freeborn. Their comments are on the page at left. (Fred R. Conrad/*The New York Times*)

There was a time when Americans thought they understood class. The upper crust vacationed in Europe and worshiped an Episcopal God. The middle class drove Ford Fairlanes, settled the San Fernando Valley, and enlisted as company men. The working class belonged to the AFL-CIO, voted Democratic, and did not take cruises to the Caribbean.

Today, the country has gone a long way toward an appearance of classlessness. Americans of all sorts are awash in luxuries that would have dazzled their grandparents. Social diversity has erased many of the old markers. It has become harder to read people's status in the clothes they wear, the cars they drive, the votes they cast, the god they worship, the color of their skin. The contours of class have blurred; some say they have disappeared.

But class is still a powerful force in American life. Over the past three decades it has come to play a greater, not lesser, role in important ways. At a time when education matters more than ever, success in school remains linked tightly to class. At a time when the country is increasingly integrated racially, the rich are isolating themselves more and more. At a time of extraordinary advances in medicine, class differences in health and life span are wide and appear to be widening.

And new research on mobility, the movement of families up and down the economic ladder, shows there is far less of it than economists once thought and less than most people believe. In fact, mobility, which once buoyed the working lives of Americans as it rose in the decades after World War II, has lately flattened out or possibly even declined, many researchers say.

Mobility is the promise that lies at the heart of the American dream. It is supposed to take the sting out of the widening gulf between the have-mores and the have-nots. There are poor and rich in the United States, of course, the argument goes; but as long as one can become the other, as long as there is something close to equality of opportunity, the differences between them do not add up to class barriers.

In the spring of 2005, *The New York Times* published a series of articles on class in America, a dimension of the national experience that tends to go unexamined, if acknowledged at all. With class now seeming more elusive than ever, the articles take stock of its influence in the lives of individuals: a lawyer who rose out of an impoverished Kentucky hollow; an unemployed metal worker in Spokane, Washington, regretting his decision to skip college; a multimillionaire in Nantucket, Massachusetts, musing over the cachet of his two-hundred-foot yacht.

The series does not purport to be all-inclusive or the last word on class. It offers no nifty formulas for pigeonholing people or decoding folkways and manners. Instead, it represents an inquiry into class as Americans encounter it: indistinct, ambiguous, the half-seen hand that upon closer examination holds some Americans down while giving others a boost.

The trends are broad and seemingly contradictory: the blurring of the landscape of class and the simultaneous hardening of certain class lines; the rise in standards of living while most people remain moored in their relative places.

Even as mobility seems to have stagnated, the ranks of the elite are opening. Today, anyone may have a shot at becoming a United States Supreme Court justice or a CEO, and there are more and more self-made billionaires. Only thirty-seven members of last year's Forbes 400, a list of the richest Americans, inherited their wealth, down from almost two hundred in the mid-1980s.

So it appears that while it is easier for a few high achievers to scale the summits of wealth, for many others it has become harder to move up from one economic class to another. Americans are arguably more likely than they were thirty years ago to end up in the class into which they were born.

A paradox lies at the heart of this new American meritocracy. Merit has replaced the old system of inherited privilege, in which parents to the manner born handed down the manor to their children. But merit, it turns out, is at least partly class-based. Parents with money, education, and connections cultivate in their children the habits that the meritocracy rewards. When their children then succeed, their success is seen as earned.

The scramble to scoop up a house in the best school district, channel a child into the right preschool program, or land the best medical specialist are all part of a quiet contest among social groups that the affluent and educated are winning in a rout.

"The old system of hereditary barriers and clubby barriers has pretty much vanished," said Eric Wanner, president of the Russell Sage Foundation, a social science research group in New York City that has published a series of studies on the social effects of economic inequality.

In place of the old system, Wanner said, have arisen "new ways of transmitting advantage that are beginning to assert themselves."

FAITH IN THE SYSTEM

Most Americans remain upbeat about their prospects for getting ahead. A recent *New York Times* poll on class found that 40 percent of Americans believed that the chance of moving up from one class to another had risen over the last thirty years, a period in which the new research shows that it has not. Thirty-five percent said it had not changed, and only 23 percent said it had dropped.

More Americans than twenty years ago believe it possible to start out poor, work hard, and become rich. They say hard work and a good education are more important to getting ahead than connections or a wealthy background.

"I think the system is as fair as you can make it," Ernie Frazier, a sixty-five-year-old real estate investor in Houston, said in an interview after participating in the poll. "I don't think life is necessarily fair. But if you persevere, you can overcome adversity. It has to do with a person's willingness to work hard, and I think it's always been that way."

Most say their standard of living is better than their parents' and imagine that their children will do better still. Even families making less than $30,000 a year subscribe to the American dream; more than half say they have achieved it or will do so.

But most do not see a level playing field. They say the very rich have too much power, and they favor the idea of class-based affirmative action to help those at the bottom. Even so, most say they oppose the government's taxing the assets a person leaves at death.

THE POLL RESULTS

To discover how Americans regard class and where they place themselves, *The New York Times* conducted a nationwide survey in March 2005. The poll uncovered optimism about social mobility. It found differences in the views of rich and poor in some areas, including the likelihood of achieving the American dream. The poll was followed by interviews with respondents, including the four people pictured at the opening of this chapter, chosen to represent different economic groups.

A Land of Opportunity

More than ever, Americans cherish the belief that it is possible to become rich. Three-quarters think the chances of moving up to a higher class are the same as or greater than thirty years ago. Still, more than half thought it unlikely that they would become wealthy. A large majority favors programs to help the poor get ahead.

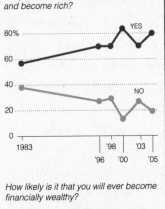

Is it possible to start out poor, work hard, and become rich?

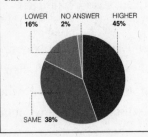

Compared with their social class when growing up, people said their current class was:

LOWER **16%** NO ANSWER **2%** HIGHER **45%**

SAME **38%**

How likely is it that you will ever become financially wealthy?

ALREADY RICH **1%** NO ANSWER **1%** SOMEWHAT **34%**

VERY **11%**

NOT AT ALL **22%**

NOT VERY **30%**

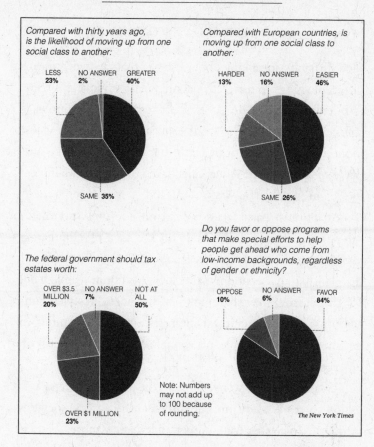

Compared with thirty years ago, is the likelihood of moving up from one social class to another:

LESS 23% | NO ANSWER 2% | GREATER 40% | SAME 35%

Compared with European countries, is moving up from one social class to another:

HARDER 13% | NO ANSWER 16% | EASIER 46% | SAME 26%

The federal government should tax estates worth:

OVER $3.5 MILLION 20% | NO ANSWER 7% | NOT AT ALL 50% | OVER $1 MILLION 23%

Do you favor or oppose programs that make special efforts to help people get ahead who come from low-income backgrounds, regardless of gender or ethnicity?

OPPOSE 10% | NO ANSWER 6% | FAVOR 84%

Note: Numbers may not add up to 100 because of rounding.

The New York Times

"They call it the land of opportunity, and I don't think that's changed much," said Diana Lackey, a sixty-year-old homemaker and wife of a retired contractor in Fulton, New York, near Syracuse. "Times are much, much harder with all the downsizing, but we're still a wonderful country."

THE ATTRIBUTES OF CLASS

One difficulty in talking about class is that the word means different things to different people. Class is rank, it is tribe, it is culture and taste. It is attitudes and assumptions, a source of identity, a system of exclusion. To some, it is just money. It is an accident of birth that can influence the outcome of a life. Some Americans barely notice it; others feel its weight in powerful ways.

At its most basic, class is one way societies sort themselves out. Even societies built on the idea of eliminating class have had stark differences in rank. Classes are groups of people of similar economic and social position; people who, for that reason, may share political attitudes, lifestyles, consumption patterns, cultural interests, and opportunities to get ahead. Put ten people in a room and a pecking order soon emerges.

When societies were simpler, the class landscape was easier to read. Marx divided nineteenth-century societies into just two classes; Max Weber added a few more. As societies grew increasingly complex, the old classes became more heterogeneous. As some sociologists and marketing consultants see it, the commonly accepted big three—the upper, middle, and working classes—have broken down into dozens of microclasses, defined by occupations or lifestyles.

A few sociologists go so far as to say that social complexity has made the concept of class meaningless. Conventional big classes have become so diverse—in income, lifestyle, political views—that they have ceased to be classes at all, said Paul W. Kingston, a professor of sociology at the University of Virginia. To him, American society is a "ladder with lots and lots of rungs."

"There is not one decisive break saying that the people below this all have this common experience," Kingston said. "Each step is equal-sized. Sure, for the people higher up this ladder, their kids are more apt to get more education, better health insurance. But that doesn't mean there are classes."

Many other researchers disagree. "Class awareness and the class language is receding at the very moment that class has reorganized American society," said Michael Hout, a professor of sociology at the University of California, Berkeley. "I find these 'end of class' discussions naïve and ironic, because we are at a time of booming inequality and this massive reorganization of where we live and how we feel, even in the dynamics of our politics. Yet people say, 'Well, the era of class is over.'"

One way to think of a person's position in society is to imagine a hand of cards. Everyone is dealt four cards, one from each suit: education, income, occupation, and wealth, the four commonly used criteria for gauging class. Face cards in a few categories may land a player in the upper middle class. At first, a person's class is his parents' class. Later, he may pick up a new hand of his own; it is likely to resemble that of his parents, but not always.

Bill Clinton traded in a hand of low cards with the help of a college education and a Rhodes scholarship and emerged decades later with four face cards. Bill Gates, who started off squarely in the upper middle class, made a fortune without finishing college, drawing three aces.

Many Americans say that they too have moved up the nation's class ladder. In the *Times* poll, 45 percent of respondents said they were in a higher class than when they grew up, while just 16 percent said they were in a lower one. Overall, 1 percent described themselves as upper class, 15 percent as upper middle class, 42 percent as middle, 35 percent as working, and 7 percent as lower.

"I grew up very poor and so did my husband," said Wanda Brown, the fifty-eight-year-old wife of a retired planner for the Puget Sound Naval Shipyard who lives in Puyallup, Washington, near Tacoma. "We're not rich but we are comfortable and we are middle class and our son is better off than we are."

THE AMERICAN IDEAL

The original exemplar of American social mobility was almost certainly Benjamin Franklin, one of seventeen children of a candle maker. About twenty years ago, when researchers first began to study mobility in a rigorous way, Franklin seemed representative of a truly fluid society, in which the rags-to-riches trajectory was the readily achievable ideal, just as the nation's self-image promised.

In a 1987 speech, Gary S. Becker, a University of Chicago economist who would later win a Nobel Prize, summed up the research by saying that mobility in the United States was so high that very little advantage was passed down from one generation to the next. In fact, researchers seemed to agree that the grandchildren of privilege and of poverty would be on nearly equal footing.

If that had been the case, the rise in income inequality beginning in the mid-1970s should not have been all that worrisome. The wealthy might have looked as if they were pulling way ahead, but if families were moving in and out of poverty and prosperity all the time, how much did the gap between the top and bottom matter?

But the initial mobility studies were flawed, economists now say. Some studies relied on children's fuzzy recollections of their parents' income. Others compared single years of income, which fluctuate considerably. Still others misread the normal progress people make as they advance in their careers, like from young lawyer to senior partner, as social mobility.

The new studies of mobility, which methodically track people's earnings over decades, have found far less movement. The economic advantage once believed to last only two or three generations is now believed to last closer to five. Mobility happens, just not as rapidly as was once thought.

"We all know stories of poor families in which the next generation did much better," said Gary Solon, a University of Michigan economist who is a leading mobility researcher. "It isn't that poor families have no chance."

But in the past, Solon added, "people would say, 'Don't worry about inequality. The offspring of the poor have

—

chances as good as the chances of the offspring of the rich.' Well, that's not true. It's not respectable in scholarly circles anymore to make that argument."

One study, by the Federal Reserve Bank of Boston, found that fewer families moved from one quintile, or fifth, of the income ladder to another during the 1980s than during the 1970s and that still fewer moved in the 1990s than in the 1980s. A study by the Bureau of Labor Statistics also found that mobility declined from the 1980s to the 1990s.

The incomes of brothers born around 1960 have followed a more similar path than the incomes of brothers born in the late 1940s, researchers at the Chicago Federal Reserve and the University of California, Berkeley, have found. Whatever children inherit from their parents—habits, skills, genes, contacts, money—seems to matter more today.

Studies on mobility over generations are notoriously difficult, because they require researchers to match the earnings records of parents with those of their children. Some economists consider the findings of the new studies murky; it cannot be definitively shown that mobility has fallen during the last generation, they say, only that it has not risen. The data will probably not be conclusive for years.

Nor do people agree on the implications. Liberals say the findings are evidence of the need for better early-education and antipoverty programs to try to redress an imbalance in opportunities. Conservatives tend to assert that mobility remains quite high, even if it has tailed off a little.

But there is broad consensus about what an optimal range of mobility is. It should be high enough for fluid

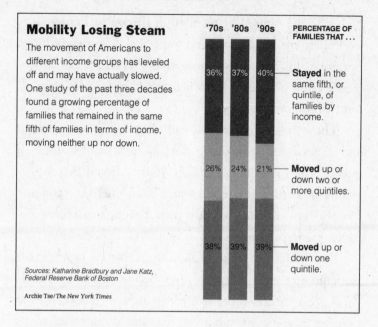

Mobility Losing Steam

The movement of Americans to different income groups has leveled off and may have actually slowed. One study of the past three decades found a growing percentage of families that remained in the same fifth of families in terms of income, moving neither up nor down.

	'70s	'80s	'90s	PERCENTAGE OF FAMILIES THAT …
	36%	37%	40%	**Stayed** in the same fifth, or quintile, of families by income.
	26%	24%	21%	**Moved** up or down two or more quintiles.
	38%	39%	39%	**Moved** up or down one quintile.

Sources: Katharine Bradbury and Jane Katz, Federal Reserve Bank of Boston

Archie Tse/*The New York Times*

movement between economic levels but not so high that success is barely tied to achievement and seemingly random, economists on both the right and left say.

As Phillip Swagel, a resident scholar at the American Enterprise Institute, put it, "We want to give people all the opportunities they want. We want to remove the barriers to upward mobility."

Yet there should remain an incentive for parents to cultivate their children. "Most people are working very hard to transmit their advantages to their children," said David I. Levine, a Berkeley economist and mobility researcher. "And that's quite a good thing."

One surprising finding about mobility is that it is not

higher in the United States than in Britain or France. It is lower here than in Canada and some Scandinavian countries but not as low as in developing countries like Brazil, where escape from poverty is so difficult that the lower class is all but frozen in place.

Those comparisons may seem hard to believe. Britain and France had hereditary nobilities; Britain still has a queen. The founding document of the United States proclaims all men to be created equal. The American economy has also grown more quickly than Europe's in recent decades, leaving an impression of boundless opportunity.

But the United States differs from Europe in ways that can gum up the mobility machine. Because income inequality is greater here, there is a wider disparity between what rich and poor parents can invest in their children. Perhaps as a result, a child's economic background is a better predictor of school performance in the United States than in Denmark, the Netherlands, or France, one study found.

"Being born in the elite in the U.S. gives you a constellation of privileges that very few people in the world have ever experienced," Levine said. "Being born poor in the U.S. gives you disadvantages unlike anything in Western Europe and Japan and Canada."

BLURRING THE LANDSCAPE

Why does it appear that class is fading as a force in American life?

For one thing, it is harder to read position in possessions. Factories in China and elsewhere churn out picture-taking cellphones and other luxuries that are now affordable to almost everyone. Federal deregulation has done the same for plane tickets and long-distance phone calls. Banks, more confident about measuring risk, now extend credit to low-income families, so that owning a home or driving a new car is no longer evidence that someone is middle class.

The economic changes making material goods cheaper have forced businesses to seek out new opportunities so that they now market to groups they once ignored. Cruise ships, years ago a symbol of the high life, have become the oceangoing equivalent of the Jersey Shore. BMW produces a cheaper model with the same insignia. Martha Stewart sells chenille jacquard drapery and scallop-embossed ceramic dinnerware at Kmart.

"The level of material comfort in this country is numbing," said Paul Bellew, executive director for market and industry analysis at General Motors. "You can make a case that the upper half lives as well as the upper 5 percent did fifty years ago."

Like consumption patterns, class alignments in politics have become jumbled. In the 1950s, professionals were reliably Republican; today they lean Democratic. Meanwhile, skilled labor has gone from being heavily Democratic to almost evenly split.

People in both parties have attributed the shift to the rise of social issues, like gun control and same-sex marriage, which have tilted many working-class voters rightward and upper-income voters toward the left. But increasing affluence

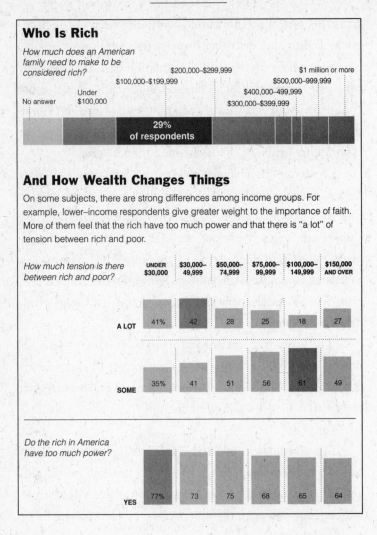

Who Is Rich

How much does an American family need to make to be considered rich?

$200,000–$299,999
$100,000–$199,999
$1 million or more
$500,000–999,999
No answer
Under $100,000
$400,000–499,999
$300,000–$399,999

29% of respondents

And How Wealth Changes Things

On some subjects, there are strong differences among income groups. For example, lower–income respondents give greater weight to the importance of faith. More of them feel that the rich have too much power and that there is "a lot" of tension between rich and poor.

How much tension is there between rich and poor?

	UNDER $30,000	$30,000– 49,999	$50,000– 74,999	$75,000– 99,999	$100,000– 149,999	$150,000 AND OVER
A LOT	41%	42	28	25	18	27
SOME	35%	41	51	56	61	49

Do the rich in America have too much power?

YES	77%	73	75	68	65	64

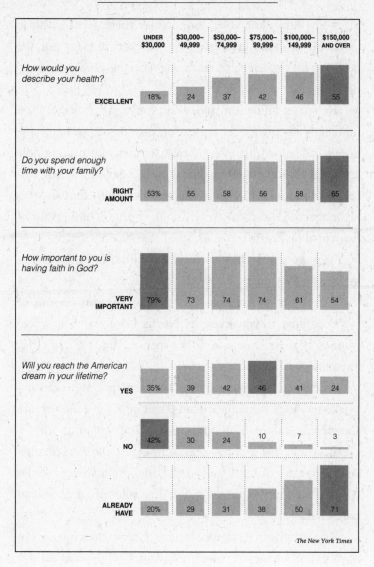

	UNDER $30,000	$30,000– 49,999	$50,000– 74,999	$75,000– 99,999	$100,000– 149,999	$150,000 AND OVER
How would you describe your health?						
EXCELLENT	18%	24	37	42	46	55
Do you spend enough time with your family?						
RIGHT AMOUNT	53%	55	58	56	58	65
How important to you is having faith in God?						
VERY IMPORTANT	79%	73	74	74	61	54
Will you reach the American dream in your lifetime?						
YES	35%	39	42	46	41	24
NO	42%	30	24	10	7	3
ALREADY HAVE	20%	29	31	38	50	71

The New York Times

plays an important role, too. When there is not only a chicken, but an organic, free-range chicken, in every pot, the traditional economic appeal to the working class can sound off-key.

Religious affiliation, too, is no longer the reliable class marker it once was. The growing economic power of the South has helped lift evangelical Christians into the middle and upper middle classes, just as earlier generations of Roman Catholics moved up in the mid-twentieth century. It is no longer necessary to switch one's church membership to Episcopal or Presbyterian as proof that one has arrived.

"You go to Charlotte, North Carolina, and the Baptists are the establishment," said Mark A. Chaves, a sociologist at the University of Arizona. "To imagine that for reasons of respectability, if you lived in North Carolina, you would want to be a Presbyterian rather than a Baptist doesn't play anymore."

The once tight connection between race and class has weakened, too, as many African-Americans have moved into the middle and upper middle classes. Diversity of all sorts—racial, ethnic, and gender—has complicated the class picture. And high rates of immigration and immigrant success stories seem to hammer home the point: The rules of advancement have changed.

The American elite, too, is more diverse than it was. The number of corporate chief executives who went to Ivy League colleges has dropped over the past fifteen years. There are many more Catholics, Jews, and Mormons in the Senate than there were a generation or two ago. Because of the economic earthquakes of the last few decades, a small but growing number of people have shot to the top.

"Anything that creates turbulence creates the opportunity for people to get rich," said Christopher S. Jencks, a professor of social policy at Harvard. "But that isn't necessarily a big influence on the 99 percent of people who are not entrepreneurs."

These success stories reinforce perceptions of mobility, as does cultural mythmaking in the form of television programs like *American Idol* and *The Apprentice*.

But beneath all that murkiness and flux, some of the same forces have deepened the hidden divisions of class. Globalization and technological change have shuttered factories, killing jobs that were once stepping-stones to the middle class. Now that manual labor can be done in developing countries for two dollars a day, skills and education have become more essential than ever.

This has helped produce the extraordinary jump in income inequality. The after-tax income of the top 1 percent of American households jumped 139 percent, to more than $700,000, from 1979 to 2001, according to the Congressional Budget Office, which adjusted its numbers to account for inflation. The income of the middle fifth rose by just 17 percent, to $43,700, and the income of the poorest fifth rose only 9 percent.

For most workers, the only time in the last three decades when the rise in hourly pay beat inflation was during the speculative bubble of the 1990s. Reduced pensions have made retirement less secure.

What It Takes to Get Ahead . . .

Hard work—more than education, natural ability, or the right connections—is regarded as crucial for getting ahead in life. While other factors can help a person's advancement, most Americans, regardless of income level, regard the individual's efforts as critical.

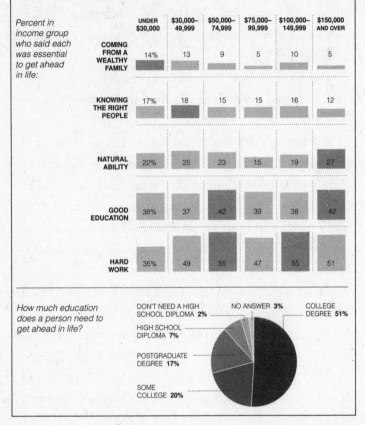

Percent in income group who said each was essential to get ahead in life:

	UNDER $30,000	$30,000–49,999	$50,000–74,999	$75,000–99,999	$100,000–149,999	$150,000 AND OVER
COMING FROM A WEALTHY FAMILY	14%	13	9	5	10	5
KNOWING THE RIGHT PEOPLE	17%	18	15	15	16	12
NATURAL ABILITY	22%	25	23	15	19	27
GOOD EDUCATION	38%	37	42	39	38	42
HARD WORK	35%	49	55	47	55	51

How much education does a person need to get ahead in life?

DON'T NEED A HIGH SCHOOL DIPLOMA **2%**

HIGH SCHOOL DIPLOMA **7%**

POSTGRADUATE DEGREE **17%**

SOME COLLEGE **20%**

NO ANSWER **3%**

COLLEGE DEGREE **51%**

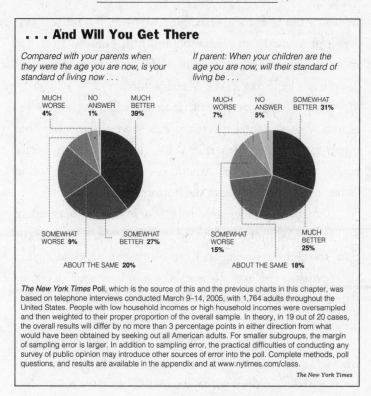

. . . And Will You Get There

Compared with your parents when they were the age you are now, is your standard of living now . . .

If parent: When your children are the age you are now, will their standard of living be . . .

MUCH WORSE 4% **NO ANSWER** 1% **MUCH BETTER** 39%

MUCH WORSE 7% **NO ANSWER** 5% **SOMEWHAT BETTER** 31%

SOMEWHAT WORSE 9% **SOMEWHAT BETTER** 27%

SOMEWHAT WORSE 15% **MUCH BETTER** 25%

ABOUT THE SAME 20%

ABOUT THE SAME 18%

The New York Times Poll, which is the source of this and the previous charts in this chapter, was based on telephone interviews conducted March 9–14, 2005, with 1,764 adults throughout the United States. People with low household incomes or high household incomes were oversampled and then weighted to their proper proportion of the overall sample. In theory, in 19 out of 20 cases, the overall results will differ by no more than 3 percentage points in either direction from what would have been obtained by seeking out all American adults. For smaller subgroups, the margin of sampling error is larger. In addition to sampling error, the practical difficulties of conducting any survey of public opinion may introduce other sources of error into the poll. Complete methods, poll questions, and results are available in the appendix and at www.nytimes.com/class.

The New York Times

Clearly, a degree from a four-year college makes even more difference than it once did. More people are getting those degrees than did a generation ago, but class still plays a big role in determining who does or does not. At 250 of the most selective colleges in the country, the proportion of students from upper-income families has grown, not shrunk.

Some colleges, worried about the trend, are adopting programs to enroll more lower-income students. One is Amherst, whose president, Anthony W. Marx, explained: "If economic mobility continues to shut down, not only will we be losing the talent and leadership we need, but we will face a risk of a society of alienation and unhappiness. Even the most privileged among us will suffer the consequences of people not believing in the American dream."

Class differences in health, too, are widening, recent research shows. Life expectancy has increased overall; but upper-middle-class Americans live longer and in better health than middle-class Americans, who live longer and in better health than those at the bottom.

Class plays an increased role, too, in determining where and with whom affluent Americans live. More than in the past, they tend to live apart from everyone else, cocooned in their exurban châteaus. Researchers who have studied census data from 1980, 1990, and 2000 say the isolation of the affluent has increased.

Family structure, too, differs increasingly along class lines. The educated and affluent are more likely than others to have their children while married. They have fewer children and have them later, when their earning power is high. On average, according to one study, college-educated women have their first child at age thirty, up from twenty-five in the early 1970s. The average age among women who have never gone to college has stayed at about twenty-two.

Those widening differences have left the educated and affluent in a superior position when it comes to investing in their children. "There is no reason to doubt the old saw that the most important decision you make is choosing your parents," said David Levine, the Berkeley economist and mobility researcher. "While it's always been important, it's probably a little more important now."

The benefits of the new meritocracy do come at a price. It once seemed that people worked hard and got rich in order to relax, but a new class marker in upper-income families is having at least one parent who works extremely long hours (and often boasts about it). In 1973, one study found, the highest-paid tenth of the country worked fewer hours than the bottom tenth. Today, those at the top work more.

In downtown Manhattan, black cars line up outside Goldman Sachs's headquarters every weeknight around nine. Employees who work that late get a free ride home, and there are plenty of them. Until 1976, a limousine waited at 4:30 p.m. to ferry partners to Grand Central Terminal. But a new management team eliminated the late-afternoon limo to send a message: four thirty is the middle of the workday, not the end.

A RAGS-TO-RICHES FAITH

Will the trends that have reinforced class lines while papering over the distinctions persist?

The economic forces that caused jobs to migrate to low-wage countries are still active. The gaps in pay, education, and health have not become a major political issue. The slicing of society's pie is more unequal than it used to be, but most Americans have a bigger piece than they or their parents once did. They appear to accept the trade-offs.

Where Do You Fit In?

The box below is a way of visualizing how income and education, two key elements of class, match up in the American population. It shows who's on top, who's at the bottom, and who's in the middle. The box on the next page shows how poll respondents described their class versus where they actually fell on the same income-education spectrum. Given a choice of five classes, the better-off poll respondents shunned the top (upper class) and the poor shunned the bottom (lower class). Most everyone placed themselves in the middle three classes: working, middle, and upper middle.

Where People Are

The shaded rectangles show the proportion of Americans over twenty-five at each income and education level.

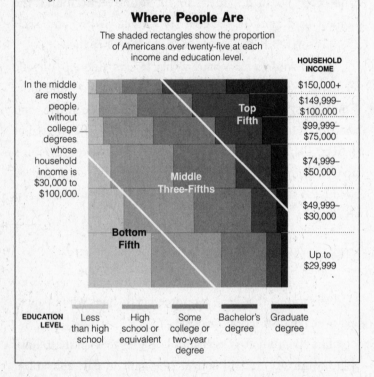

In the middle are mostly people without college degrees whose household income is $30,000 to $100,000.

HOUSEHOLD INCOME

$150,000+
$149,999–$100,000
$99,999–$75,000
$74,999–$50,000
$49,999–$30,000
Up to $29,999

Top Fifth

Middle Three-Fifths

Bottom Fifth

EDUCATION LEVEL

| Less than high school | High school or equivalent | Some college or two-year degree | Bachelor's degree | Graduate degree |

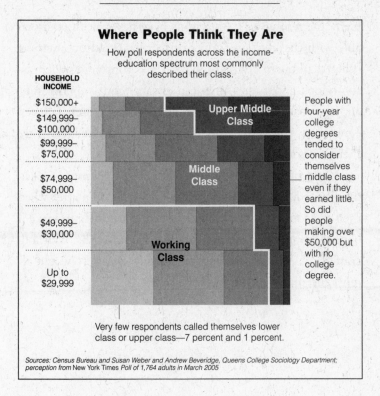

Where People Think They Are

How poll respondents across the income-education spectrum most commonly described their class.

HOUSEHOLD INCOME

- $150,000+
- $149,999–$100,000
- $99,999–$75,000
- $74,999–$50,000
- $49,999–$30,000
- Up to $29,999

Upper Middle Class

Middle Class

Working Class

People with four-year college degrees tended to consider themselves middle class even if they earned little. So did people making over $50,000 but with no college degree.

Very few respondents called themselves lower class or upper class—7 percent and 1 percent.

Sources: Census Bureau and Susan Weber and Andrew Beveridge, Queens College Sociology Department; perception from New York Times Poll of 1,764 adults in March 2005

Faith in mobility, after all, has been consciously woven into the national self-image. Horatio Alger's books have made his name synonymous with rags-to-riches success, but that was not his personal story. He was a second-generation Harvard man, who became a writer only after losing his Unitarian ministry because of allegations of sexual misconduct. Ben Franklin's autobiography was punched up after his death to underscore his rise from obscurity.

The idea of fixed class positions, on the other hand, rubs

many the wrong way. Americans have never been comfortable with the notion of a pecking order based on anything other than talent and hard work. Class contradicts their assumptions about the American dream, equal opportunity, and the reasons for their own successes and even failures. Americans, constitutionally optimistic, are disinclined to see themselves as stuck.

Blind optimism has its pitfalls. If opportunity is taken for granted, as something that will be there no matter what, then the country is less likely to do the hard work to make it happen. But defiant optimism has its strengths. Without confidence in the possibility of moving up, there would almost certainly be fewer success stories.

2. Life at the Top in America Isn't Just Better, It's Longer

Janny Scott

Jean G. Miele's recovery after a heart attack benefited from the support of family and friends. (James Estrin/*The New York Times*)

Jean G. Miele's heart attack happened on a sidewalk in Midtown Manhattan in May 2004. He was walking back to work along Third Avenue with two colleagues after a several-hundred-dollar sushi lunch. There was the distant rumble of heartburn, the ominous tingle of perspiration. Then Miele, an architect, collapsed onto a concrete planter in a cold sweat.

Will L. Wilson's heart attack came four days earlier in the bedroom of his brownstone in Bedford-Stuyvesant in Brooklyn. He had been regaling his fiancée with the details of an all-you-can-eat dinner he was beginning to regret. Wilson, a Consolidated Edison office worker, was feeling a little bloated. He flopped onto the bed. Then came a searing sensation, like a hot iron deep inside his chest.

Ewa Rynczak Gora's first signs of trouble came in her rented room in the noisy shadow of the Brooklyn-Queens Expressway. It was the Fourth of July. Gora, a Polish-born housekeeper, was playing bridge. Suddenly she was sweating, stifling an urge to vomit. She told her husband not to call an ambulance; it would cost too much. Instead, she tried a home remedy: salt water, a double dose of hypertension pills, and a glass of vodka.

Architect, utility worker, maid: heart attack is the great leveler, and in those first fearful moments, three New Yorkers with little in common faced a single common threat. But in the months that followed, their experiences diverged. Social class—that elusive combination of income, education, occupation, and wealth—played a powerful role in Miele's, Wilson's, and Gora's struggles to recover.

Class informed everything from the circumstances of their heart attacks to the emergency care each received, the households they returned to, and the jobs they hoped to resume. It shaped their understanding of their illness, the support they got from their families, their relationships with their doctors. It helped define their ability to change their lives and shaped their odds of getting better.

Class is a potent force in health and longevity in the United States. The more education and income people have, the less likely they are to have and die of heart disease, strokes, diabetes, and many types of cancer. Upper-middle-class Americans live longer and in better health than middle-class Americans, who live longer and better than those at the bottom. And the gaps are widening, say people who have researched social factors in health.

As advances in medicine and disease prevention have increased life expectancy in the United States, the benefits have disproportionately gone to people with education, money, good jobs, and connections. They are almost invariably in the best position to learn new information early, modify their behavior, take advantage of the latest treatments, and have the cost covered by insurance.

Many risk factors for chronic diseases are now more common among the less educated than the better educated. Smoking has dropped sharply among the better educated, but not among the less. Physical inactivity is more than twice as common among high school dropouts as among college graduates. Lower-income women are more likely than other women to be overweight, though the pattern among men may be the opposite.

There may also be subtler differences. Some researchers now believe that the stress involved in so-called high-demand, low-control jobs further down the occupational scale is more harmful than the stress of professional jobs that come with greater autonomy and control. Others are studying the health impact of job insecurity, lack of support on the job, and employment that makes it difficult to balance work and family obligations.

Then there is the issue of social networks and support, the differences in the knowledge, time, and attention that a person's family and friends are in a position to offer. What is the effect of social isolation? Neighborhood differences have also been studied: How stressful is a neighborhood? Are there safe places to exercise? What are the health effects of discrimination?

Heart attack is a window on the effects of class on health. The risk factors—smoking, poor diet, inactivity, obesity, hypertension, high cholesterol, and stress—are all more common among the less educated and less affluent, the same group that research has shown is less likely to receive cardiopulmonary resuscitation, to get emergency room care, or to adhere to lifestyle changes after heart attacks.

"In the last twenty years, there have been enormous advances in rescuing patients with heart attack and in knowledge about how to prevent heart attack," said Ichiro Kawachi, a professor of social epidemiology at the Harvard School of Public Health. "It's like diffusion of innovation: whenever innovation comes along, the well-to-do are much quicker at adopting it. On the lower end, various disadvantages have piled onto the poor. Diet has gotten worse. There's a lot more work stress. People have less time, if they're poor, to devote to health maintenance behaviors when they are juggling two jobs. Mortality rates even among the poor are coming down, but the rate is not anywhere near as fast as for the well-to-do. So the gap has increased."

Bruce G. Link, a professor of epidemiology and socio-medical sciences at Columbia University, said of the double-edged consequences of progress: "We're creating disparities. It's almost as if it's transforming health, which used to be like fate, into a commodity. Like the distribution of BMWs or goat cheese."

THE BEST OF CARE

Jean Miele's advantage began with the people he was with on May 6, when the lining of his right coronary artery rup-tured, cutting off the flow of blood to his sixty-six-year-old heart. His two colleagues were knowledgeable enough to dismiss his request for a taxi and call an ambulance instead.

And because he was in Midtown Manhattan, there were major medical centers nearby, all licensed to do the latest in emergency cardiac care. The emergency medical technician in the ambulance offered Miele a choice. He picked Tisch Hospital, part of New York University Medical Center, an academic center with relatively affluent patients, and passed up Bellevue, a city-run hospital with one of the busiest emergency rooms in New York.

Within minutes, Miele was on a table in the cardiac catheterization laboratory, awaiting angioplasty to unclog his artery—a procedure that many cardiologists say has be-come the gold standard in heart attack treatment. When he developed ventricular fibrillation, a heart rhythm abnormal-ity that can be fatal within minutes, the problem was quickly fixed.

Then Dr. James N. Slater, a fifty-four-year-old cardiologist with some twenty-five thousand cardiac catheterizations under his belt, threaded a catheter through a small incision in the top of Miele's right thigh and steered it toward his heart. Miele lay on the table, thinking about dying. By 3:52 p.m., less than two hours after Miele's first symptoms, his artery was reopened and Slater implanted a stent to keep it that way.

Time is muscle, as cardiologists say. The damage to Miele's heart was minimal.

Miele spent just two days in the hospital. His brother-in-law, a surgeon, suggested a few specialists. His brother, Joel, chairman of the board of another hospital, asked his hospital's president to call New York University. "Professional courtesy," Joel Miele explained later. "The bottom line is that someone from management would have called patient care and said, 'Look, would you make sure everything's okay?' "

Things went less flawlessly for Will Wilson, a fifty-three-year-old transportation coordinator for Con Ed. He imagined fleetingly that he was having a bad case of indigestion, though he had had a heart attack before. His fiancée insisted on calling an ambulance. Again, the emergency medical technician offered a choice of two nearby hospitals—neither of which had state permission to do angioplasty, the procedure Jean Miele received.

Wilson chose the Brooklyn Hospital Center over Woodhull Medical and Mental Health Center, the city-run hospital that serves three of Brooklyn's poorest neighborhoods. At Brooklyn Hospital, he was given a drug to break up the clot blocking an artery to his heart. It worked at first, said Narinder P. Bhalla, the hospital's chief of cardiology, but the clot re-formed.

So Bhalla had Wilson taken to the Weill Cornell Center of New York–Presbyterian Hospital in Manhattan the next morning. There, Bhalla performed angioplasty and implanted a stent. Asked later whether Wilson would have been better off if he had had his heart attack elsewhere, Bhalla said the most important issue in heart attack treatment was getting the patient to a hospital quickly.

But he added, "In his case, yes, he would have been better off had he been to a hospital that was doing angioplasty."

Wilson spent five days in the hospital before heading home on many of the same high-priced drugs that Miele would be taking and under similar instructions to change his diet and exercise regularly. After his first heart attack, in 2000, he quit smoking; but once he was feeling better, he stopped taking several medications, drifted back to red meat and fried foods, and let his exercise program slip.

This time would be different, he vowed: "I don't think I'll survive another one."

Ewa Gora's experience was the rockiest. First, she hesitated before allowing her husband to call an ambulance; she hoped her symptoms would go away. He finally insisted; but when the ambulance arrived, she resisted leaving. The emergency medical technician had to talk her into going. She was given no choice of hospitals; she was simply taken to Woodhull, the city hospital Will Wilson had rejected.

Woodhull was busy when Gora arrived around 10:30

p.m. A triage nurse found her condition stable and classified her as "high priority." Two hours later, a physician assistant and an attending doctor examined her again and found her complaining of chest pain, shortness of breath, and heart palpitations. Over the next few hours, tests confirmed she was having a heart attack.

She was given drugs to stop her blood from clotting and to control her blood pressure, treatment that Woodhull officials say is standard for the type of heart attack she was having. The heart attack passed. The next day, Gora was transferred to Bellevue, the hospital Jean Miele had turned down, for an angiogram to assess her risk of a second heart attack.

But Gora, who was fifty-nine at the time, came down with a fever at Bellevue, so the angiogram had to be canceled. She remained at Bellevue for two weeks, being treated for an infection. Finally, she was sent home. No angiogram was ever done.

COMFORTS AND RISKS

Jean Miele is a member of New York City's upper middle class. The son of an architect and an artist, he worked his way through college, driving an ice-cream truck and upholstering theater seats. He spent two years in the military and then joined his father's firm, where he built a practice as not only an architect but also an arbitrator and an expert witness, developing real estate on the side.

Miele is the kind of person who makes things happen.

He bought a $21,000 house in the Park Slope section of Brooklyn, sold it about fifteen years later for $285,000, and used the money to build his current house next door, worth over $2 million. In Brookhaven, on Long Island, he took a derelict house on a single acre, annexed several adjoining lots, and created what is now a four-acre, three-house compound with an undulating lawn and a fifteen-thousand-square-foot greenhouse he uses as a workshop for his collection of vintage Jaguars.

Miele's architecture partners occasionally joked that he was not in the business for the money, which to some extent was true. He had figured out how to live like a millionaire, he liked to say, even before he became one. He had worked four-day weeks for twenty years, spending long weekends with his family, sailing or iceboating on Bellport Bay and re-building cars.

Miele had never thought of himself as a candidate for a heart attack—even though both his parents had died of heart disease; even though his brother had had arteries unclogged; and even though he himself was on hypertension medication, his cholesterol levels bordered on high, and his doctor had been suggesting he lose weight.

He was a passionate chef who put great store in the healthfulness of fresh ingredients from the Mieles' vegetable garden or the greengrocers in Park Slope. His breakfasts may have been a cardiologist's nightmare—eggs, sausage, bacon, pastina with a poached egg—but he considered his marinara sauce to be healthy perfection: just garlic, oil, tomatoes, salt, and pepper.

He figured he had something else working in his favor: he was happy. He adored his second wife, Lori, twenty-three years younger, and their six-year-old daughter, Emma. He lived within blocks of his two sisters and two of his three grown children from his first marriage. The house regularly overflowed with guests, including Miele's former wife and her husband. He seemed to know half the people of Park Slope.

"I walk down the street and I feel good about it every day," Miele, a gregarious figure with twinkling blue eyes and a taste for worn T-shirts and jeans, said of his neighborhood. "And yes, that gives me a feeling of well-being."

His approach to his health was utilitarian. When body parts broke, he got them fixed so he could keep doing what he liked to do. So he had had disk surgery, rotator cuff surgery, surgery for a carpal tunnel problem. But he was also not above an occasional bit of neglect. In March 2004, his doctor suggested a stress test after Miele complained of shortness of breath. On May 6, the prescription was still hanging on the kitchen cabinet door.

An important link in the safety net that caught Miele was his wife, a former executive at a sweater manufacturing company who had stopped work to raise Emma but managed the Mieles' real estate as well. While Miele was still in the hospital, she was on the Internet, Googling stents.

She scheduled his medical appointments. She got his prescriptions filled. Leaving him at home one afternoon, she taped his cardiologist's business card to the couch where he was sitting. "Call Dr. Hayes and let him know you're coughing," she said, her fingertips on his shoulder. Thirty minutes later, she called home to check.

She prodded Miele, gently, to cut his weekly egg consumption to two, from seven. She found fresh whole wheat pasta and cooked it with turkey sausage and broccoli rabe. She knew her way around nutrition labels.

Lori Miele took on the burden of dealing with the hospital and insurance companies. She accompanied her husband to his doctor's appointments and retained pharmaceutical dosages in her head.

"I can just leave and she can give you all the answers to all the questions," Miele said to his cardiologist, Dr. Richard M. Hayes, one day.

"Okay, why don't you just leave?" Hayes said back. "Can she also examine you?"

With his wife's support, Miele set out to lose thirty pounds. His pasta consumption plunged to a plate a week from two a day. It was not hard to eat healthfully from the Mieles' kitchens. Even the "junk drawer" in Park Slope was stocked with things like banana chips and sugared almonds. Lunches in Brookhaven went straight from garden to table: tomatoes with basil, eggplant, corn, zucchini flower tempura.

At his doctor's suggestion, Miele enrolled in a three-month monitored exercise program for heart disease patients, called cardiac rehab, which has been shown to reduce the mortality rate among heart patients by 20 percent. Miele's insurance covered the cost. He even managed to minimize the inconvenience, finding a class ten minutes from his country house.

He had the luxury of not having to rush back to work. By early June, he had decided he would take the summer off, and maybe cut back his workweek when he returned to the firm.

"You know, the more I think about it, the less I like the idea of going back to work," he said. "I don't see any real advantage. I mean, there's money. But you've got to take the money out of the equation."

So he put a new top on his 1964 Corvair. He played host to a large family reunion, replaced the heat exchanger in his boat, and transformed the ramshackle greenhouse into an elaborate workshop. His weight dropped to 189 pounds, from 211. He had doubled the intensity of his workouts. His blood pressure was lower than ever.

Miele saw Hayes only twice in six months, for routine follow-ups. He had been known to walk out of doctors' offices if he was not seen within twenty minutes, but Hayes did not keep him waiting. The Mieles were swept into the examining room at the appointed hour. Buoyed by the evidence of Miele's recovery, they would head out to lunch in downtown Manhattan. Those afternoons had the feel of impromptu dates.

"My wife tells me that I'm doing fourteen-hour days," Miele mused one afternoon, slicing cold chicken and piling it with fresh tomatoes on toast. "She said, 'You're doing better now than you did ten years ago.' And I said, 'I haven't had sex in a week.' And she said, 'Well?' "

Just one unpleasant thing happened. Miele's partners informed him in late July that they wanted him to retire. It caught him off guard, and it hurt. He countered by taking the position that he was officially disabled and therefore entitled to be paid for a full year after he began his medical leave. "I mean, the guy has a heart attack," he said later. "So you get him while he's down?"

LUKEWARM EFFORTS TO REFORM

Will Wilson fits squarely in the city's middle class. His parents had been sharecroppers who moved north and became a machinist and a nurse. He grew up in Bedford-Stuyvesant and had spent thirty-four years at Con Ed. He had an income of $73,000, five weeks' vacation, health benefits, a house worth $450,000, and plans to retire to North Carolina when he is fifty-five.

Wilson, too, had imagined becoming an architect. But there had been no money for college, so he found a job as a utility worker. By age twenty-two, he had two children. He considered going back to school, with the company's support, to study engineering. But doing shift work, and with small children, he never found the time.

For years he was a high-voltage cable splicer, a job he loved because it meant working outdoors with plenty of freedom and overtime pay. But on a snowy night in the early 1980s, a car skidded into a stanchion, which hit him in the back. A doctor suggested that Wilson learn to live with the pain instead of having disk surgery, as Jean Miele had done.

So Wilson became a laboratory technician, then a transportation coordinator, working in a cubicle in a low-slung building in Astoria, Queens, overseeing fuel deliveries for the company's fleet. Some people might think of the work as tedious, Wilson said, "but it keeps you busy."

"Sometimes you look back over your past life experiences and you realize that if you would have done something different, you would have been someplace else," he said. "I don't dwell on it too much because I'm not in a negative position. But you do say, 'Well, dag, man, I should have done this or that.'"

Wilson's health was not bad, but far from perfect. He had quit drinking and smoking, but had high cholesterol, hypertension, and diabetes. He was slim, five foot nine, and just under 170 pounds. He traced his first heart attack to his smoking, his diet, and the stress from a grueling divorce.

His earlier efforts to reform his eating habits were half-hearted. Once he felt better, he stopped taking his cholesterol and hypertension drugs. When his cardiologist moved and referred Wilson to another doctor, he was annoyed by what he considered the rudeness of the office staff. Instead of demanding courtesy or finding another specialist, Wilson stopped going.

By the time Dr. Bhalla encountered Wilson at Brooklyn Hospital, there was damage to all three main areas of his heart. Bhalla prescribed a half-dozen drugs to lower Wilson's cholesterol, prevent clotting, and control his blood pressure.

"He has to behave himself," Bhalla said. "He needs to be more compliant with his medications. He has to really go on a diet, which is grains, no red meat, no fat. No fat at all."

Wilson had grown up eating his mother's fried chicken,

pork chops, and macaroni and cheese. He confronted those same foods at holiday parties and big events. There were doughnut shops and fried chicken places in his neighborhood; but Wilson's fiancée, Melvina Murrell Green, found it hard to find fresh produce and good fish.

"People in my circle, they don't look at food as, you know, too much fat in it," Wilson said. "I don't think it's going to change. It's custom."

At Red Lobster after his second heart attack, Green would order chicken and Wilson would have salmon—plus a side order of fried shrimp. "He's still having a problem with the fried seafood," Green reported sympathetically.

Whole grains remained mysterious. "That we've got to work on," she said. "Well, we recently bought a bag of grain something. I'm not used to that. We try to put it on the cereal. It's okay."

In August 2004, Green's blood pressure shot up. The culprit turned out to be a turkey chili recipe that she and Wilson had discovered: every ingredient except the turkey came from a can. She was shocked when her doctor pointed out the salt content. The Con Ed cafeteria, too, was problematic. So Wilson began driving to the Best Yet Market in Astoria at lunch to troll the salad bar.

Dr. Bhalla had suggested that Wilson walk for exercise. There was little open space in the neighborhood, so Wilson and Green often drove just to go for a stroll. In the fall of 2004 he entered a cardiac rehab program like Miele's, only less convenient. He would drive into Manhattan after work, during the afternoon rush, three days a week. He would hunt for on-street parking or pay too much for a space in a lot. Then a stranger threatened to damage Wilson's car in a confrontation over a free spot, so Wilson switched to the subway.

For a time, he considered applying for permanent disability. But Con Ed allowed him to return to work "on restrictions," so he decided to go back, with plans to retire in a year and a half. The week before he went back, he and Green took a seven-day cruise to Nassau. It was a revelation.

"Sort of like helped me to see there's a lot more things to do in life," he said. "I think a lot of people deny themselves certain things in life, in terms of putting things off, 'I'll do it later.' Later may never come."

IGNORING THE RISKS

Ewa Gora is a member of the working class. A bus driver's daughter, she arrived in New York City from Kraków in the early 1990s, leaving behind a grown son. She worked as a housekeeper in a residence for the elderly in Manhattan, making beds and cleaning toilets. She said her income was $21,000 to $23,000 a year, with health insurance through her union.

For $365 a month, she rented a room in a friend's Brooklyn apartment on a street lined with aluminum-sided row houses and American flags. She used the friend's bathroom and kitchen. She was in her seventh year on a waiting list for a subsidized one-bedroom apartment in the adjacent Williamsburg neighborhood. In the meantime, she had acquired a roommate: Edward Gora, an asbestos-removal worker newly arrived from Poland and ten years her junior, whom she met and married in 2003.

Like Jean Miele, Ewa Gora had never imagined she was at risk of a heart attack, though she was overweight, hypertensive, and a thirty-year smoker, and heart attacks had killed her father and sister. She had numerous health problems, which she addressed selectively, getting treated for back pain, ulcers, and so on, until the treatment became too expensive or inconvenient, or her insurance declined to pay.

"My doctor said, 'Ewa, be careful with cholesterol,'" recalled Gora, whose vestigial Old World sense of propriety had her dressed in heels and makeup for every visit to Bellevue. "When she said that, I think nothing; I don't care. Because I don't believe this touch me. Or I think she have to say like that because she doctor. Like cigarettes: she doctor, she always told me to stop. And when I got out of the office, lights up."

Gora had a weakness for the peak of the food pyramid. She grew up on her mother's fried pork chops, spare ribs, and meatballs—all cooked with lard—and had become a pizza, hamburger, and french fry enthusiast in the United States. Fast food was not only tasty but also affordable. "I eat terrible," she reported cheerily from her bed at Bellevue. "I like grease food and fast food. And cigarettes."

She loved the feeling of a cigarette between her fingers, the rhythmic rise and fall of it to her lips. Using her home computer, she had figured out how to buy Marlboros online for just $2.49 a pack. Her husband smoked, her friends all smoked. Everyone she knew seemed to love tobacco and steak.

Her life was physically demanding. She would rise at 6:00 a.m. to catch a bus to the subway, change trains three times, and arrive at work by 8:00 a.m. She would make twenty-five to thirty beds, vacuum, cart out trash. Yet she says she loved her life. "I think America is El Dorado," she said. "Because in Poland now is terrible; very little bit money. Here, I don't have a lot of, but I live normal. I have enough, not for rich life but for normal life."

The precise nature of Gora's illness was far from clear to her even after two weeks in Bellevue. In her first weeks home, she remained unconvinced that she had had a heart attack. She arrived at the Bellevue cardiology clinic for her first follow-up appointment imagining that whatever procedure had earlier been canceled would then be done, that it would unblock whatever was blocked, and that she would be allowed to return to work.

Jad Swingle, a doctor completing his specialty training in cardiology, led Gora through the crowded waiting room and into an examining room. She clutched a slip of paper with words she had translated from Polish using her pocket dictionary: "dizzy," "groin," "perspiration." Swingle asked her questions, speaking slowly. Do you ever get chest discomfort? Do you get short of breath when you walk?

She finally interrupted: "Doctor, I don't know what I have, why I was in hospital. What is this heart attack? I don't know why I have this. What I have to do to not repeat this?"

No one had explained these things, Gora believed. Or,

she wondered, had she not understood? She perched on the examining table, ankles crossed, reduced by the setting to an oversize, obedient child. Swingle examined her, then said he would answer her questions "in a way you'll understand." He set about explaining heart attacks: the narrowed artery, the blockage, the partial muscle death.

Gora looked startled.

"My muscle is dead?" she asked.

Swingle nodded.

What about the procedure that was never done?

"I'm not sure an angiogram would help you," he said. She needed to stop smoking, take her medications, walk for exercise, come back in a month.

"My muscle is still dead?" she asked again, incredulous.

"Once it's dead, it's dead," Swingle said. "There's no bringing it back to life."

Outside, Gora tottered toward the subway, fourteen blocks away, on pink high-heeled sandals in 89-degree heat. "My thinking is black," she said, uncharacteristically glum. "Now I worry. You know, you have hand? Now I have no finger."

If Jean Miele's encounters with the health care profession in the first months after his heart attack were occasional and efficient, Ewa Gora's were the opposite. Whereas he saw his cardiologist just twice, Gora, burdened by complications, saw hers a half-dozen times. Meanwhile, her heart attack seemed to have shaken loose a host of other problems.

A growth on her adrenal gland had turned up on a Bellevue CAT scan, prompting a visit to an endocrinologist. An old knee problem flared up; an orthopedist recommended surgery. An alarming purple rash on her leg led to a trip to a dermatologist. Because of the heart attack, she had been taken off hormone replacement therapy and was constantly sweating. She tore open a toe stepping into a pothole and needed stitches.

Without money or connections, moderate tasks consumed entire days. One cardiology appointment coincided with a downpour that paralyzed the city. Gora was supposed to be at the hospital laboratory at 8:00 a.m. to have blood drawn and back at the clinic at 1:00 p.m. In between, she wanted to meet with her boss about her disability payments. She had a 4:00 p.m. appointment in Brooklyn for her knee.

So at 7:00 a.m., she hobbled through the rain to the bus to the subway to another bus to Bellevue. She was waiting outside the laboratory when it opened. Then she took a bus uptown in jammed traffic, changed buses, descended into the subway at Grand Central Terminal, rode to Times Square, found service suspended because of flooding, climbed the stairs to Forty-second Street, maneuvered through angry crowds hunting for buses, and found another subway line.

She reached her workplace an hour and a half after leaving Bellevue; if she had had the money she could have made the trip in twenty minutes by cab. Her boss was not there. So she returned to Bellevue and waited until 2:35 p.m. for her one o'clock appointment. As always, she asked Dr. Swingle to let her return to work. When he insisted she have a stress test first, a receptionist gave her the first available appointment—seven weeks away.

Meanwhile, Gora was trying to stop smoking. She had quit in the hospital, then returned home to a husband and a neighbor who both smoked. To be helpful, her husband smoked in the shared kitchen next door. He was gone most of the day, working double shifts. Alone and bored, Gora started smoking again, then called Bellevue's free smoking cessation program and enrolled.

For the next few months, she trekked regularly to "the smoking department" at Bellevue. A counselor supplied her with nicotine patches and advice, not always easy for her to follow: stay out of the house; stay busy; avoid stress; satisfy oral cravings with, say, candy. The counselor suggested a support group, but Gora was too ashamed of her English to join. Even so, over time her tobacco craving waned.

There was just one hitch: Gora was gaining weight. To avoid smoking, she was eating. Her work had been her exercise and now she could not work. Dr. Swingle suggested cardiac rehab, leaving it up to Gora to find a program and arrange it. Gora let it slide. As for her diet, she had vowed to stick to chicken, turkey, lettuce, tomatoes, and low-fat cottage cheese. But she got tired of that. She began sneaking cookies when no one was looking—and no one was.

She cooked separate meals for her husband, who was not inclined to change his eating habits. She made him meatballs with sauce, liver, soup from spare ribs. Then one day she helped herself to one of his fried pork chops, and was soon eating the same meals he was. As an alternative to eating cake while watching television, she turned to pistachios, and then ate a pound in a single sitting.

Cruising the 99 Cent Wonder store in Williamsburg, where the freezers were filled with products like Budget Gourmet Rigatoni with Cream Sauce, she pulled down a small package of pistachios: two and a half servings, thirteen grams of fat per serving. "I can eat five of these," she confessed, ignoring the nutrition label. Not servings. Bags.

Heading home after a trying afternoon in the office of the apartment complex in Williamsburg, where the long-awaited apartment seemed perpetually just out of reach, Gora slipped into a bakery and emerged with a doughnut, her first since her heart attack. She found a park bench where she had once been accustomed to reading and smoking. Working her way through the doughnut, confectioners' sugar snowing onto her chest, she said ruefully, "I miss my cigarette."

She wanted to return to work. She felt uncomfortable depending on her husband for money. She worried that she was becoming indolent and losing her English. Her disability payments, for which she needed a doctor's letter every month, came to just half of her $331 weekly salary. Once, she spent hours searching for the right person at Bellevue to give her a letter, only to be told to come back in two days.

The copayments on her prescriptions came to about eighty dollars each month. Unnerving computer printouts from the pharmacist began arriving: "Maximum benefit reached." She switched to her husband's health insurance plan. Twice, Bellevue sent bills for impossibly large amounts of money for services her insurance was supposed to cover. Both times she spent hours traveling into Manhattan to the hospital's business office to ask why she had been billed. Both times a clerk listened, made a phone call, said the bill was a mistake, and told her to ignore it.

When the stress test was finally done, Dr. Swingle said the results showed she was not well enough to return to full-time work. He gave her permission for part-time work, but her boss said it was out of the question. By November, four months after her heart attack, her weight had climbed to 197 pounds from 185 in July. Her cholesterol levels were stubbornly high and her blood pressure was up, despite drugs for both.

In desperation, Gora embarked upon a curious, heart-unhealthy diet clipped from a Polish-language newspaper. Day 1: two hardboiled eggs, one steak, one tomato, spinach, lettuce with lemon and olive oil. Another day: coffee, grated carrots, cottage cheese, and three containers of yogurt. Yet another: just steak. She decided not to tell her doctor. "I worry if he don't let me, I not lose the weight," she said.

UNEVEN RECOVERIES

Nearly a year after his heart attack, Jean Miele was, remarkably, better off. He had lost thirty-four pounds and was exercising five times a week and taking subway stairs two at a time. He had retired from his firm on the terms he wanted. He was working from home, billing $225 an hour. More money in less time, he said. His blood pressure and cholesterol were low. "You're doing great," Dr. Hayes had said. "You're doing better than ninety-nine percent of my patients."

—

Will Wilson's heart attack had been a setback. His heart function remained impaired, though improved somewhat. At one checkup in the spring of 2005, his blood pressure and his weight had been a little high. He still enjoyed fried shrimp on occasion, but he took his medications diligently. He graduated from cardiac rehab with plans to join a health club with a pool. And he was looking forward to retirement.

Ewa Gora's life and health were increasingly complex. With Dr. Swingle's reluctant approval, she returned to work in November 2004. She had moved into the subsidized apartment in Williamsburg, which gave her her own kitchen and bathroom for the first time in seven years. But she began receiving menacing phone calls from a collection agency about an old bill her health insurance had not covered. Her husband, with double pneumonia, was out of work for weeks.

She had her long-awaited knee surgery in January 2005. But it left her temporarily unable to walk. Her weight hit two hundred pounds. When the diet failed, she considered another consisting largely of fruit and vegetables sprinkled with an herbal powder. Her blood pressure and cholesterol remained ominously high. She had been warned that she was now a borderline diabetic.

"You're becoming a full-time patient, aren't you?" Swingle remarked.

3. A Marriage of Unequals

TAMAR LEWIN

Cate Woolner, seated at right, and her sons live with her husband of six years, Dan Croteau, in Northfield, Massachusetts. (Suzanne DeChillo/*The New York Times*)

When Dan Croteau met Cate Woolner six years ago, he was selling cars at the Keene, New Hampshire, Mitsubishi lot and she was pretending to be a customer, test-driving a black Montero while she and her eleven-year-old son, Jonah, waited for their car to be serviced.

The test-drive lasted an hour and a half. Jonah got to see how the vehicle performed in off-road mud puddles. And Croteau and Woolner hit it off so well that she later sent him a note, suggesting that if he was not involved with someone, not a Republican, and not an alien life-form, maybe they could meet for coffee. Croteau dithered about the propriety of dating a customer, but when he finally responded, they talked on the phone from ten at night until five in the morning.

They had a lot in common. Each had two failed marriages and two children. Both loved dancing, motorcycles, Bob Dylan, bad puns, liberal politics, and National Public Radio.

But when they began dating, they found differences, too. The religious difference—he is Roman Catholic, she is Jewish—posed no problem. The real gap between them, both said, was more subtle: Croteau came from the working class, and Woolner from money.

Croteau, who turned fifty in 2005, grew up in Keene, an old mill town in southern New Hampshire. His father was a factory worker whose education ended at the eighth grade; his mother had some factory jobs, too. Croteau had a difficult childhood and quit school at sixteen. He then left home, joined the navy, and drifted through a long series of jobs without finding any real calling. He married his pregnant nineteen-year-old girlfriend and had two daughters, Lael and Maggie, by the time he was twenty-four.

"I was raised in a family where my grandma lived next door, my uncles lived on the next road over, my dad's two brothers lived next to each other, and I pretty much played with my cousins," he said. "The whole concept of life was that you should try to get a good job in the factory. My mother tried to encourage me. She'd say, 'Dan's bright; ask him a question.' But if I'd said I wanted to go to college, it would have been like saying I wanted to grow gills and breathe underwater."

He always felt that the rich people in town, "the ones with their names on the buildings," as he put it, lived in another world.

Woolner, who is fifty-four, comes from that other world. The daughter of a doctor and a dancer, she grew up in a comfortable home in Hartsdale, New York, with the summer camps, vacations, and college education that wealthy Westchester County families can take for granted. She was always uncomfortable with her money; when she came into a modest inheritance at twenty-one, she ignored the monthly bank statements for several years, until she learned to channel her unease into philanthropy benefiting social causes. She was in her mid-thirties and married to a psychotherapist when Isaac and Jonah were born.

"My mother's father had a Rolls-Royce and a butler and a second home in Florida," Woolner said, "and from as far back as I can remember, I was always aware that I had more than other people, and I was uncomfortable about it because it didn't feel fair. When I was little, what I fixated on with my girlfriends was how I had more pajamas than they did. So when I'd go to birthday sleepovers, I'd always take them a pair of pajamas as a present."

Marriages that cross class boundaries may not present as obvious a set of challenges as those that cross the lines of race or nationality. But in a quiet way, people who marry across class lines are also moving outside their comfort zones, into the uncharted territory of partners with a different level of wealth and education, and often, a different set of assumptions about things like manners, food, child-rearing, gift-giving, and how to spend vacations. In cross-class marriages, one partner will usually have more money, more options, and, almost inevitably, more power in the relationship.

It is not possible to say how many cross-class marriages there are. But to the extent that education serves as a proxy for class, they seem to be declining. Even as more people marry across racial and religious lines, often to partners who match them closely in other respects, fewer are choosing partners with a different level of education. While most of those marriages used to involve men marrying women with less education, studies have found, lately that pattern has flipped, so that by 2000, the majority involved women, like Cate Woolner, marrying men with less schooling—the combination most likely to end in divorce.

"It's definitely more complicated, given the cultural scripts we've all grown up with," said Woolner, who has a master's degree in counseling and radiates a thoughtful sincerity. "We've all been taught it's supposed to be the man who has the money and the status and the power."

BIAS ON BOTH SIDES

When he met Woolner, Dan Croteau had recently stopped drinking and was looking to change his life. But when she told him, soon after they began dating, that she had money, it did not land as good news.

"I wished she had waited a little," Croteau said. "When she told me, my first thought was, uh oh, this is a complication. From that moment I had to begin questioning my motivations. You don't want to feel like a gold digger. You have to tell yourself, here's this person that I love, and here's this quality that comes with the package. Cate's very generous, and she thinks a lot about what's fair and works very hard to level things out, but she also has a lot of baggage around that quality. She has all kinds of choices I don't have. And she does the lion's share of the decision making."

Before introducing Woolner to his family, Croteau warned them about her background. "I said, 'Mom, I want you to know Cate and her family are rich,'" he recalled. "And she said, 'Well, don't hold that against her; she's probably very nice anyway.' I thought that was amazing."

There were biases on the other side, too. Just last summer, Croteau said, when they were at Woolner's mother's house on Martha's Vineyard, his mother-in-law confessed to him that she had initially been embarrassed that he was a car salesman and worried that her daughter was taking him on as a kind of do-good project.

Still, the relationship moved quickly. Croteau met Woolner in the fall of 1998 and moved into her comfortable home in Northfield, Massachusetts, the next spring, after meeting her condition that he sell his gun.

Even before Croteau moved in, Woolner gave him money to buy a new car and pay off some debts. "I wanted to give him the money," she said. "I hadn't sweated it. I told him that this was money that had just come to me for being born into one class, while he was born into another class." And when he lost his job not long after, Woolner began paying him a monthly stipend—he sometimes refers to it as an allowance—that continued, at a smaller level, until she quit her long-standing job at a local antipoverty agency. She also agreed to pay for a $10,000 computer course that helped prepare him for his current job as a software analyst at the Cheshire Medical Center in Keene. From the beginning, the balance of power in the relationship was a sufficiently touchy issue that at Woolner's urging, a few months before their wedding in August 2001, they joined a series of workshops on cross-class relationships.

"I had abject terror at the idea of the group," said Croteau, who is blunt and intellectually engaging. "It's certainly an upper-class luxury to pay to tell someone your troubles, and with all the problems in the world, it felt a little strange to sit around talking about your relationship. But it was useful. It was a relief to hear people talk about the same kinds of issues we were facing, about who had power in the relationship and how they used it. I think we would have made it anyway, but we would have had a rockier time without the group."

It is still accepted truth within the household that Woolner's status has given her the upper hand in the marriage. At dinner one night, when her son Isaac said baldly, "I always think of my mom as having the power in the relationship," Croteau did not flinch. He is fully aware that in this relationship he is the one whose life has been most changed.

CONFUSING DIFFERENCES

The Woolner-Croteau household is just up the hill from the groomed fields of Northfield Mount Hermon prep school—a constant local reminder to Dan Croteau of just how differently his wife's sons and his daughters have been educated. Jonah is now a senior there. Isaac, who also attended the school, is now back at Lewis & Clark College in Oregon after taking a couple of semesters away to study in India and to attend massage school while working in a deli near home.

By contrast, Croteau's adult daughters—who have never lived with the couple—made their way through the Keene public schools.

"I sometimes think Jonah and Isaac need a dose of reality, that a couple years in public school would have shown them something different," Croteau said. "On the other hand I sometimes wish I'd been able to give Maggie and Lael what they had. My kids didn't have the same kind of privilege and the same kind of schools. They didn't have teachers concerned about their tender growing egos. It was catch-as-catch-can for them, and that still shows in their personalities."

Croteau had another experience of Northfield Mount Hermon as well. He briefly had a job as its communications manager, but could not adjust to its culture.

"There were all these Ivy Leaguers," he said. "I didn't understand their nuances, and I didn't make a single friend there. In working-class life, people tell you things directly, they're not subtle. At NMH, I didn't get how they did things. When a vendor didn't meet the deadline, I called and said,

'Where's the job?' When he said, 'We bumped you, we'll have it next week,' I said, 'What do you mean, next week? We have a deadline, you can't do business like that.' It got back to my supervisor, who came and said, 'We don't yell at vendors.' The idea seemed to be that there weren't deadlines in that world, just guidelines."

Croteau said he was far more comfortable at the hospital. "I deal mostly with nurses and other computer nerds and they come from the same kind of world I do, so we know how to talk to each other," he said.

But in dealing with Woolner's family, especially during the annual visits to Martha's Vineyard, Croteau said, he sometimes finds himself back in class bewilderment, feeling again that he does not get the nuances. "They're incredibly gracious to me, very well bred and very nice," he said, "so much so that it's hard to tell whether it's sincere, whether they really like you."

Croteau still seems impressed by his wife's family, and their being among "the ones with their names on the buildings." It is he who shows a visitor the framed print of the old Woolner Distillery in Peoria, Illinois, and, describing the pictures on the wall, mentions that this in-law went to Yale, and that one knew Gerald Ford.

FAMILY DIVISIONS

Croteau and Woolner are not the only ones aware of the class divide within the family; so are the two sets of children.

Money is continually tight for Lael Croteau, who is in

graduate school in educational administration at the University of Vermont, and Maggie, who is working three jobs while in her second year of law school at American University. At restaurants, they ask to have the leftovers wrapped to take home.

Neither could imagine taking a semester off to try out massage school, as Isaac did. They are careful about their manners, their plans, their clothes.

"Who's got money, who doesn't, it's always going on in my head," Maggie said. "So I put on the armor. I have the bag. I have the shirt. I know people can't tell my background by looking."

The Croteau daughters are the only ones among twelve first cousins who made it to college. Most of the others married and had babies right after high school.

"They see us as different, and sometimes that can hurt," Maggie said.

The daughters walk a fine line. They are deeply attached to their mother, who did most of their rearing, but they are also attracted to the Woolner world and its possibilities. Through holidays and Vineyard vacations, they have come to feel close not only to their stepbrothers, but also to Cate Woolner's sisters' children, whose pictures are on display in Lael's house in Vermont. And they see, up close, just how different their upbringing was.

"Jonah and Isaac don't have to worry about how they dress, or whether they'll have the money to finish college, or anything," Lael said. "That's a real luxury. And when one of the little kids asks, 'Why do people sneeze?' their mom will say, 'I don't know; that's a great question. Let's go to the museum, and check it out.' My mom is very smart and certainly engages us on many levels, but when we asked a difficult question, she'd say, 'Because I said so.'"

The daughters' lives have been changed not only by Woolner's warm, stable presence, but also by her gifts of money for snow tires or books, the family vacations she pays for, and her connections. One of Woolner's cousins, a Washington lawyer, employs Maggie both at her office and as a house sitter.

For Woolner's sons, Dan Croteau's arrival did not make nearly as much difference. They are mostly oblivious of the extended Croteau family, and have barely met the Croteau cousins, who are close to their age and live nearby but lead quite different lives. Indeed, in early February, while Isaac Woolner was readjusting to college life, Croteau's nephew, another twenty-year-old Isaac who had enlisted in the Marines right after high school, was shot in the face in Falluja, Iraq, and shipped to Bethesda Medical Center in Maryland. Isaac and Jonah are easygoing young men, neither of whom has any clear idea what he wants to do in life. "For a while I've been trying to find my passion," Jonah said. "But I haven't been passionately trying to find my passion."

Isaac fantasizes about opening a brewery-cum-performance-space, traveling through South America, or operating a sunset massage cruise in the Caribbean. He knows he is on such solid ground that he can afford fantasy.

"I have the most amazing safety net a person could have," he said, "incredible, loving, involved, and wealthy parents."

On the rare occasions when they are all together, the daughters get on easily with the sons, though there are occasional tensions. Maggie would love to have a summer internship with a human rights group, but she needs paid work, and when she graduates, with more than $100,000 of debt, she will need a law firm job, not one with a nonprofit. So when Isaac one day teased her as being a sellout, she reminded him that it was a lot easier to live your ideals when you did not need to make money to pay for them.

And there are moments when the inequalities within the family are painfully obvious.

"I do feel the awkwardness of helping Isaac buy a car, when I'm not helping them buy a car," Cate Woolner said of the daughters. "We've talked about that. But I also have to be aware of overstepping. Their mother's house burned down, which was awful for them and for her and I really wanted to help. I took out my checkbook and I didn't know what was appropriate. In the end I wrote a check for fifteen hundred dollars. Emily Post doesn't deal with these situations."

She and Croteau remain conscious of the class differences between them, and the ways in which their lives have been shaped by different experiences.

On one visit to New York City, where Woolner's mother lives in the winter, Woolner lost her debit card and felt anxious about being disconnected, even briefly, from her money.

For Croteau, it was a strange moment. "She had real discomfort, even though we were around the corner from her mother, and she had enough money to do anything we were likely to do, assuming she wasn't planning to buy a car or a diamond all of a sudden," he said. "So I didn't understand the problem. I know how to walk around without a safety net. I've done it all my life."

Both he and his wife express pride that their marriage has withstood its particular problems and stresses.

"I think we're always both amazed that we're working it out," Woolner said.

But almost from the beginning they agreed on an approach to their relationship, a motto now engraved inside their wedding rings: "Press on regardless."

4. Up from the Holler:
Living in Two Worlds, at Home in Neither

TAMAR LEWIN

Della Mae Justice returned to her Appalachian hometown after law school. (Suzanne DeChillo/*The New York Times*)

Della Mae Justice stands before the jury in the Pike County Courthouse, arguing that her client's land in Greasy Creek Hollow was illegally grabbed when the neighbors expanded their cemetery behind her home.

With her soft Appalachian accent, Justice leaves no doubt that she is a local girl, steeped in the culture of the old family cemeteries that dot the mountains here in East Kentucky. "I grew up in a holler, I surely did," she tells jurors as she lays out the boundary conflict.

Justice is, indeed, a product of the Appalachian coal-mining country where lush mountains flank rust-colored creeks, the hollows rising so steeply that there is barely room for a house on either side of the creeks. Her family was poor, living for several years in a house without indoor plumbing. Her father was absent; her older half brother sometimes had to hunt squirrels for the family to eat. Her mother married again when Della was nine. But the stepfather, a truck driver, was frequently on the road, and her mother, who was mentally ill, often needed the young Della to care for her.

Justice was always hungry for a taste of the world beyond the mountains. Right after high school, she left Pike County, making her way through college and law school, spending time in France, Scotland, and Ireland, and beginning a high-powered legal career. In just a few years she moved up the ladder from rural poverty to the high-achieving circles of the middle class.

Now, at thirty-four, she is back home. But her journey has transformed her so thoroughly that she no longer fits in easily. Her change in status has left Justice a little off balance, seeing the world from two vantage points at the same time: the one she grew up in and the one she occupies now.

Far more than people who remain in the social class they are born to, surrounded by others of the same background, Justice is sensitive to the cultural significance of the cars people drive, the food they serve at parties, where they go on vacation—all the little clues that indicate social status. By every conventional measure, Justice is now solidly middle class, but she is still trying to learn how to feel middle class. Almost every time she expresses an idea, or explains herself, she checks whether she is being understood, asking, "Does that make sense?"

"I think class is everything, I really do," she said recently. "When you're poor and from a low socioeconomic group, you don't have a lot of choices in life. To me, being from an upper class is all about confidence. It's knowing you have choices, knowing you set the standards, knowing you have connections."

BROKEN TIES

In Pikeville, the site of the Hatfield-McCoy feud (Della Mae Justice is a Hatfield), memories are long and family roots mean a lot. Despite her success, Justice worries about what people might remember about her, especially about the time when she was fifteen and her life with her mother and stepfather imploded in violence, sending her into foster care for a wretched nine months.

"I was always in the lowest socioeconomic group," she said, "but foster care ratcheted it down another notch. I hate that period of my life, when for nine months I was a child with no family."

While she was in foster care, Justice lived in one end of a double-wide trailer, with the foster family on the other end. She slept alongside another foster child, who wet the bed, and every morning she chose her clothes from a box of hand-me-downs. She was finally rescued when her father heard about her situation and called his nephew, Joe Justice.

Joe Justice was thirty-five years older than Della Mae, a successful lawyer who lived in the other Pikeville, one of the well-to-do neighborhoods on the mountain ridges. He and his wife, Virginia, had just built a four-bedroom contemporary home, complete with a swimming pool, on Cedar Gap Ridge.

Joe Justice had never even met his cousin until he saw her in the trailer, but afterward he told his wife that it was "abhorrent" for a close relative to be in foster care. While poverty is common around Pikeville, foster care is something much worse: a sundering of the family ties that count for so much. So Joe and Virginia Justice took Della Mae in. She changed schools, changed address—changed worlds, in effect—and moved into an octagonal bedroom downstairs from the Justices' two-year-old son.

"The shock of going to live in wealth, with Joe and Virginia, it was like Little Orphan Annie going to live with the Rockefellers," Della Mae Justice said. "It was not easy. I was shy and socially inept. For the first time, I could have had the right clothes, but I didn't have any idea what the right clothes were. I didn't know much about the world, and I was always afraid of making a wrong move. When we had a school trip for chorus, we went to a restaurant. I ordered a club sandwich, but when it came with those toothpicks on either end, I didn't know how to eat it, so I just sat there, staring at it and starving, and said I didn't feel well."

Joe and Virginia Justice worried about Della Mae's social

unease and her failure to mingle with other young people in their church. But they quickly sensed her intelligence and encouraged her to attend Berea College, a small liberal arts institution in Kentucky that accepts students only from low-income families. Tuition is free and everybody works. For Della Mae, as for many other Berea students, the experience of being one among many poor people, all academically capable and encouraged to pursue big dreams, was life-altering.

It was at Berea that Justice met the man who became her husband, Troy Price, the son of a tobacco farmer with a sixth-grade education. They married after graduation, and when Justice won a fellowship, the couple went to Europe for a year of independent travel and study. When Justice won a scholarship to the University of Kentucky law school in Lexington, Price went with her, to graduate school in family studies.

After graduating fifth in her law school class, Justice clerked for a federal judge, then joined Lexington's largest law firm, where she put in long hours in hopes of making partner. She and her husband bought a town house, took trips, ate in restaurants almost every night, and spent many Sunday afternoons at real estate open houses in Lexington's elegant older neighborhoods. By all appearances, they were on the fast track.

But Justice still felt like an outsider. Her coeditors on the law review, her fellow clerks at the court, and her colleagues at the law firm all seemed to have a universe of information that had passed her by. She saw it in matters big and small—the casual references, to Che Guevara or Mount Vesuvius, that meant nothing to her; the food at dinner parties that she would not eat because it looked raw in the middle.

"I couldn't play Trivial Pursuit, because I had no general knowledge of the world," she said. "And while I knew East Kentucky, they all knew a whole lot about Massachusetts and the Northeast. They all knew who was important, whose father was a federal judge. They never doubted that they had the right thing to say. They never worried about anything."

Most of all, they all had connections that fed into a huge web of people with power. "Somehow, they all just knew each other," she said.

KNITTING A NEW FAMILY

Justice's life took an abrupt turn in 1999, when her half brother, back in Pike County, called out of the blue to say that his children, Will and Anna Ratliff, who had been living with their mother, were in foster care. Justice and her brother had not been close, and she had met the children only once or twice, but the call was impossible to ignore. As her cousin Joe had years earlier, she found it intolerable to think of her flesh and blood in foster care.

So over the next year, Della Mae Justice and her husband got custody of both children and went back to Pikeville, only 150 miles away but far removed from their life in Lexington. The move made all kinds of sense. Will and Anna, thirteen and twelve, could stay in touch with their mother and father. Troy Price got a better job, as executive director of Pikeville's new support center for abused children. Justice went to work for her cousin at his law firm, where a flexible schedule allowed her to look after the two children.

And yet for Justice the return to Pikeville has been almost as dislocating as moving out of foster care and into that octagonal bedroom all those years ago. On a rare visit recently to the hollows where she used to live, she was moved to tears when a neighbor came out, hugged her, and told her how he used to pray and worry for her and how happy he was that she had done so well. But mostly, she winces when reminded of her past.

"Last week, I picked up the phone in my office," she recalled, "and the woman said who she was, and then said, 'You don't remember me, do you?' And I said, 'Were you in foster care with me?' That was crazy. Why would I do that? It's not something I advertise, that I was in care."

While most of her workweek is devoted to commercial law, Justice spends Mondays in family court, representing families with the kind of problems hers had. She bristles whenever she runs into any hint of class bias, or the presumption that poor people in homes heated by kerosene or without enough bedrooms cannot be good parents.

"The norm is, people that are born with money have money, and people who weren't don't," she said recently. "I know that. I know that just to climb the three inches I have, which I've not gone very far, took all of my effort. I have worked hard since I was a kid and I've done nothing but work to try and pull myself out."

The class a person is born into, she said, is the starting point on the continuum. "If your goal is to become, on a national scale, a very important person, you can't start way back on the continuum, because you have too much to make up in one lifetime. You have to make up the distance you can in your lifetime so that your kids can then make up the distance in their lifetime."

COMING TO TERMS WITH LIFE

Justice is still not fully at ease in the other, well-to-do Pikeville, and in many ways she and her husband had to start from scratch in finding a niche there. Church is where most people in town find friends and build their social life. But Justice and Price had trouble finding a church that was a comfortable fit; they went through five congregations, starting at the Baptist church she had attended as a child and ending up at the Disciples of Christ, an inclusive liberal church with many affluent members. The pastor and his wife, transplants to Kentucky, have become their closest friends. Others have come more slowly.

"Partly the problem is that we're young, for middle-class people, to have kids as old as Will and Anna," Justice said. "And the fact that we're raising a niece and nephew, that's kind of a flag that we weren't always middle class, just like saying you went to Berea College tells everyone you were poor."

And though in terms of her work Justice is now one of Pikeville's leading citizens, she is still troubled by the old doubts and insecurities. "My stomach's always in knots getting ready to go to a party, wondering if I'm wearing the right thing, if I'll know what to do," she said. "I'm always thinking: How does everybody else know that? How do they know how to act? Why do they all seem so at ease?"

A lot of her energy now goes into Will and Anna. She wants to bring them up to have the middle-class ease that still eludes her. "Will and Anna know what it's like to be poor, and now we want them to be able to be just regular kids," she said. "When I was young, I always knew who were the kids at school with the involved parents that brought in the cookies, and those were the kids who got chosen for every special thing, not ones like me, who got free lunch and had to borrow clothes from their aunt if there was a chorus performance."

Because Justice is self-conscious about her teeth—"the East Kentucky overbite," she says ruefully—she made sure early on that Anna got braces. She worries about the children's clothes as much as her own. "Everyone else seems to know when the khaki pants the boys need are on sale at JCPenney," she said. "I never know these things."

As a child, Justice never had the resources for her homework projects. So when Anna was assigned to build a Navajo hogan, they headed to Wal-Mart for supplies.

"We put in extra time, so she would appear like those kids with the involved parents," Justice said. "I know it's just a hogan, but making a project that looks like the other kids' projects is part of fitting in."

Justice encouraged Will to join the Boy Scouts, and when he was invited to join his school's Academic Team, which competes in quiz bowls, she insisted that he try it. When he asked her whether he might become a drug addict if he took the medicine prescribed for him, she told him it was an excellent question, and at the doctor's office prompted him to ask the doctor directly. She nudges both children to talk about what happens in school, to recount the plots of the books they read, and to discuss current events.

It is this kind of guidance that distinguishes middle-class children from children of working-class and poor families, according to sociologists who have studied how social class affects child-rearing. While working-class parents usually teach their children, early on, to do what they are told without argument and to manage their own free time, middle-class parents tend to play an active role in shaping their children's activities, seeking out extracurricular activities to build their talents, and encouraging them to speak up and even to negotiate with authority figures.

Justice's efforts are making a difference. Will found that he enjoyed Academic Team. Anna now gets evening phone calls from several friends. Both have begun to have occasional sleepovers. And gradually, Justice is coming to terms with her own life. On New Year's Eve, after years in a modest rented town house, she and her husband moved into a new house that reminds her of the *Brady Bunch* home. It has four bedrooms and a swimming pool. In a few years, when her older cousin retires, Justice will most likely take over the practice, a solid prospect, though far less lucrative, and less glamorous, than a partnership at her Lexington law firm.

"I've worked very hard all my life—to have a life that's not so far from where I started out," she said. "It is different, but it's not the magical life I thought I'd get."

5. On a Christian Mission to the Top

LAURIE GOODSTEIN AND DAVID D. KIRKPATRICK

Tim Havens, right, and Jan Vezikov in Manning Chapel at Brown University, where Havens leads a morning prayer session. (Fred R. Conrad/*The New York Times*)

For a while during the winter of 2004–5, Tim Havens, a recent graduate of Brown University and then an evangelical missionary there, had to lead his morning prayer group in a stairwell of the campus chapel. That was because workers were clattering in to remake the lower floor for a display of American Indian art, and a Buddhist student group was chanting in the small sanctuary upstairs.

Like most of the Ivy League universities, Brown was founded by Protestant ministers as an expressly Christian college. But over the years it gradually shed its religious affiliation and became a secular institution, as did the other Ivies. In addition to Buddhists, the Brown chaplain's office now recognizes "heathen/pagan" as a "faith community."

But these days evangelical students like those in Havens's prayer group are becoming a conspicuous presence at Brown. Of a student body of 5,700, about 400 participate in one of three evangelical student groups—more than the number of active mainline Protestants, the campus chaplain says. And these students are in the vanguard of a larger social shift not just on campuses but also at golf resorts and in boardrooms; they are part of an expanding beachhead of evangelicals in the American elite.

The growing power and influence of evangelical Christians is manifest everywhere these days, from the bestseller lists to the White House, but in fact their share of the general population has not changed much in half a century. Most pollsters agree that people who identify themselves as white evangelical Christians make up about a quarter of the population, just as they have for decades.

What has changed is the class status of evangelicals— Protestants who emphasize the authority of the Bible, the importance of a "born-again" conversion experience, and spreading the faith. In 1929, the theologian H. Richard Niebuhr described born-again Christianity as the "religion of the disinherited." But over the last forty years, evangelicals have pulled steadily closer in income and education to

mainline Protestants in the historically affluent establishment denominations. In the process they have overturned
the old social pecking order in which "Episcopalian," for example, was a code word for upper class, and "fundamental-
ist" or "evangelical" shorthand for lower. Evangelicals are
now increasingly likely to be college graduates and in the top
income brackets. Evangelical CEOs pray together on monthly
conference calls, evangelical investment bankers study the
Bible over lunch on Wall Street, and deep-pocketed evangelical donors gather at golf courses for conferences restricted
to those who give more than $200,000 annually to Christian
causes.

Their growing wealth and education help explain the
new influence of evangelicals in American culture and politics. Their buying power fuels the booming market for
Christian books, music, and films. Their rising income has
paid for construction of vast megachurches in suburbs across
the country. Their charitable contributions finance dozens
of mission agencies, religious broadcasters, and international
service groups.

On *The Chronicle of Philanthropy*'s latest list of the four
hundred top charities, Campus Crusade for Christ, an evangelical student group, raised more from private donors than
the Boy Scouts of America, the Public Broadcasting Service,
and Easter Seals.

Now a few affluent evangelicals are directing their attention and money at some of the tallest citadels of the secular
elite: Ivy League universities. Three years ago a group of
evangelical Ivy League alumni formed the Christian Union,

an organization intended to "reclaim the Ivy League for Christ," according to its fund-raising materials, and to "shape the hearts and minds of many thousands who graduate from these schools and who become the elites in other American cultural institutions."

The Christian Union has bought and maintains new evangelical student centers at Brown, Princeton, and Cornell, and has plans to establish a center on every Ivy League campus. In April 2005, 450 students, alumni, and supporters met in Princeton for an "Ivy League Congress on Faith and Action." A keynote speaker was Charles W. Colson, the born-again Watergate felon turned evangelical thinker.

Matt Bennett, founder of the Christian Union, told the conference, "I love these universities—Princeton and all the others, my alma mater, Cornell—but it really grieves me and really hurts me to think of where they are now."

The Christian Union's immediate goal, he said, was to recruit campus missionaries. "What is happening now is good," Bennett said, "but it is like a finger in the dike of keeping back the flood of immorality."

And trends in the Ivy League today could shape the culture for decades to come, he said. "So many leaders come out of these campuses. Seven of the nine supreme court justices are Ivy League grads; four of the seven Massachusetts Supreme Court justices; Christian ministry leaders; so many presidents, as you know; leaders of business—they are everywhere."

He added, "If we are going to change the world, we have got, by God's power, to see these campuses radically changed."

AN OUTSIDER ON CAMPUS

Tim Havens, who graduated from Brown in 2004, is the kind of missionary the Christian Union hopes to enlist. An evangelical from what he calls a "solidly middle class" family in the Midwest, he would have been an anomaly at Brown a couple of generations ago. He applied there, he said, out of a sense of "nonconformity" and despite his mother's preference that he attend a Christian college.

"She just was nervous about, and rightfully so, what was going to happen to me freshman year," Havens recalled.

When he arrived at Brown, in Providence, Rhode Island, Havens was astounded to find that the biggest campus social event of the fall was the annual SexPowerGod dance, sponsored by the Lesbian Gay Bisexual Transgender Queer Alliance and advertised with dining-hall displays depicting pairs of naked men or women. "Why do they have to put God in the name?" he said. "It seems kind of disrespectful."

Havens found himself a double outsider of sorts. In addition to being devoted to his faith, he was a scholarship student at a university where half the students can afford $45,000 in tuition and fees without recourse to financial aid and where, he said, many tend to "spend money like water."

But his modest means did not stand out as much as his efforts to guard his morals. He did not drink, and he almost never cursed. And he was determined to stay "pure" until marriage, though he did not lack for attention from female students. Just as his mother feared, Havens, a broad-shouldered former wrestler with tousled brown hair and a guileless smile, wavered some his freshman year and dated several classmates.

"I was just like, 'Oh, I can get this girl to like me,'" he recalled. "'Oh, she likes me; she's cute.' And so it was a lot of fairly short and meaningless relationships. It was pretty destructive."

In his sophomore year, though, his evangelical a cappella singing group, a Christian twist on an old Ivy League tradition, interceded. With its support, he rededicated himself to serving God, and by his senior year he was running his own Bible-study group, hoping to inoculate first-year students against the temptations he had faced. They challenged one another, Havens said, "committing to remain sexually pure, both in a physical sense and in avoiding pornography and ogling women and like that."

Havens is now living in a house owned and supported by the Christian Union and is trying to reach not just other evangelicals but nonbelievers as well.

PRAYERS IN THE BOARDROOMS

The Christian Union is the brainchild of forty-year-old Matt Bennett, who earned bachelor's and master's degrees at Cornell and later directed the Campus Crusade for Christ at Princeton. Bennett, tall and soft-spoken with a Texas drawl that waxes and wanes depending on the company he is in, said he got the idea during a forty-day water-and-juice fast, when he heard God speaking to him one night in a dream.

"He was speaking to me very strongly that he wanted to

see an increasing and dramatic spiritual revival in a place like Princeton," Bennett said.

While working for Campus Crusade, Bennett discovered that it was hard to recruit evangelicals to minister to the elite colleges of the Northeast because the environment was alien to them and the campuses often far from their homes. He also found that the evangelical ministries were hobbled without adequate salaries to attract professional staff members and without centers of their own where students could gather, socialize, and study the Bible. Jews had Hillel Houses, and Roman Catholics had Newman Centers.

He thought evangelicals should have their own houses, too, and began a furious round of fund-raising to buy or build some. An early benefactor was his twin brother, Monty, who had taken over the Dallas hotel empire their father built from a single Holiday Inn and who donated a three-story Victorian in a neighborhood near Brown.

To raise more money, Bennett has followed a grapevine of affluent evangelicals around the country, winding up even in places where evangelicals would have been a rarity just a few decades ago. In Manhattan, for example, he visited Wall Street boardrooms and met with the founder of Socrates in the City, a roundtable for religious intellectuals that gathers monthly at places like the Algonquin Hotel and the Metropolitan Club.

Those meetings introduced him to an even more promising pool of like-minded Christians, the New Canaan Group, a Friday morning prayer breakfast typically attended by more than a hundred investment bankers and other professionals. The breakfasts started in the Connecticut home of a partner in Goldman Sachs but grew so large they had to move to a local church. Like many other evangelicals, some members attend churches that adhere to evangelical doctrine but that remain affiliated with mainline denominations.

Other donors to the Christian Union are members of local elites across the Bible Belt. For example, Bennett paid a visit to Montgomery, Alabama, for lunch with Julian L. McPhillips Jr., a wealthy Princeton alumnus and the managing partner of a local law firm. Bennett, wearing an orange Princeton tie, said he wanted to raise enough money for the Christian Union to hire someone to run a "healing ministry" for students with depression, eating disorders, or drug or alcohol addiction.

McPhillips, who shares Bennett's belief in the potential of faith healing, remarked that he had once cured an employee's migraine headaches just by praying for him. "We joke in my office that we don't need health insurance," he told Bennett before writing a check for $1,000.

Bennett's database has grown to about five thousand names gathered by word of mouth alone. They are mostly Ivy League graduates whose regular alumni contributions he hopes to channel into the Christian Union. And these Ivy League evangelicals, in turn, are just a small fraction of the large number of their affluent fellow believers.

GAINING ON THE MAINLINE

Their commitment to their faith is confounding a long-held assumption that, like earlier generations of Baptists or Pentecostals, prosperous evangelicals would abandon their religious ties or trade them for membership in establishment churches. Instead, they have kept their traditionalist beliefs, and their churches have even attracted new members from among the well-off.

Meanwhile, evangelical Protestants are pulling closer to their mainline counterparts in class and education. As late as 1965, for example, a white mainline Protestant was two and a half times as likely to have a college degree as a white evangelical, according to an analysis by Professor Corwin E. Smidt, a political scientist at Calvin College, an evangelical institution in Grand Rapids, Michigan. But by 2000, a mainline Protestant was only 65 percent more likely to have the same degree. And since 1985, the percentage of incoming freshmen at highly selective private universities who said they were born-again also rose by half, to 11 or 12 percent each year from 7.3 percent, according to the Higher Education Research Institute at the University of California, Los Angeles.

To many evangelical Christians, the reason for their increasing worldly success and cultural influence is obvious: God's will at work. Some also credit leaders like the mid-century intellectual Carl F. H. Henry, who helped found a large and influential seminary, a glossy evangelical Christian magazine, and the National Association of Evangelicals, a powerful umbrella group that now includes fifty-one denominations. Henry and his followers implored believers to look beyond their churches and fight for a place in the American mainstream.

There were also demographic forces at work, beginning with the GI Bill, which sent a pioneering generation of evangelicals to college. Probably the greatest boost to the prosperity of evangelicals as a group came with the Sun Belt expansion of the 1970s and the Texas oil boom, which brought new wealth and businesses to the regions where evangelical churches had been most heavily concentrated.

The most striking example of change in how evangelicals see themselves and their place in the world may be the Assemblies of God, a Pentecostal denomination. It was founded in Hot Springs, Arkansas, in 1914, by rural and working-class Christians who believed that the Holy Spirit had moved them to speak in tongues. Shunned by established churches, they became a sect of outsiders, and their preachers condemned worldly temptations like dancing, movies, jewelry, and swimming in public pools. But like the Southern Baptists and other conservative denominations, the Assemblies gradually dropped their separatist strictures as their membership prospered and spread.

As the denomination grew, Assemblies preachers began speaking not only of heavenly rewards but also of the material blessings God might provide in this world. The notion was controversial in some evangelical circles but became widespread nonetheless, and it made the Assemblies' faith more compatible with an upwardly mobile middle class.

By the 1970s, Assemblies churches were sprouting up in affluent suburbs across the country. Recent surveys by Margaret Poloma, a historian at the University of Akron in Ohio, found Assemblies members more educated and better off than the general public.

As they flourished, evangelical entrepreneurs and strivers built a distinctly evangelical business culture of prayer meetings, self-help books, and business associations. In some cities outside the Northeast, evangelical business owners list their names in Christian Yellow Pages.

The rise of evangelicals has also coincided with the gradual shift of most of them from the Democratic Party to the Republican and their growing political activism. The conservative Christian political movement seldom developed in poor, rural Bible Belt towns. Instead, its wellsprings were places like the Reverend Ed Young's booming megachurch in suburban Houston or the Reverend Timothy LaHaye's in Orange County, California, where evangelical professionals and businesspeople had the wherewithal to push back against the secular culture by organizing boycotts, electing school board members, and lobbying for conservative judicial appointments.

"A BUNCH OF HEATHENS"

Tim Havens, the Brown missionary, is part of the upsurge of well-educated born-again Christians. He grew up in one of the few white households in a poor black neighborhood of St. Louis, where his parents had moved to start a church, which failed to take off. Havens's father never graduated from college. After being laid off from his job at a marketing company in 2003, he now works in an insurance company's software and systems department. Havens's mother home-schooled the family's six children for at least a few years each.

Havens got through Brown on scholarships and loans, and at graduation was $25,000 in debt. To return to campus for his missionary year and pay his expenses, he needed to raise an additional $36,000, and on the advice of Geoff Freeman, the head of the Brown branch of Campus Crusade, he did his fund-raising in St. Louis.

"It is easy to sell New England in the Midwest," as Freeman put it later. Midwesterners, he said, see New Englanders as "a bunch of heathens."

So Havens drove home each day from a summer job at a stone supply warehouse to work the phone from his cluttered childhood bedroom. He told potential donors that many of the American-born students at Brown had never even been to church, to say nothing of the students from Asia or the Middle East. "In a sense, it is pre-Christian," he explained.

Among his family's friends, however, encouragement was easier to come by than cash. As the summer came to a close, Havens was still $6,000 short. He decided to give himself a pay cut and go back to Brown with what he had raised, trusting God to take care of his needs just as he always had when money seemed scarce during college.

"God owns the cattle on a thousand hills," he often told himself. "God has plenty of money."

Thanks to the Christian Union, Havens's present quarters as a ministry intern at Brown are actually more upscale than his home in St. Louis. On Friday nights, he is a host for a Bible-study and dinner party for seventy or eighty Christian students, who serve themselves heaping plates of pasta before breaking into study groups. Afterward, they regroup in the living room for board games and goofy improvisation contests, all free of profanity and even double entendre.

Lately, though, Havens has been contemplating steps that would take him away from Brown and campus ministry. After a chaste romance—"I didn't kiss her until I asked her to marry me," he said—he became engaged to a missionary colleague, Liz Chalmers. He has been thinking about how to support the children they hope to have.

And he has been considering the example of his future father-in-law, Daniel Chalmers, a Baptist missionary to the Philippines who ended up building power plants there and making a small fortune. Chalmers has been a steady donor to Christian causes, and he bought a plot of land in Oregon, where he plans to build a retreat center.

"God has always used wealthy people to help the church," Havens said. He pointed out that in the Bible, rich believers helped support the apostles, just as donors to the Christian Union are investing strategically in the Ivy League today.

With those examples and his own father in mind, Havens chose medicine over campus ministry. He scored well on his medical school entrance exams and, after another year at Brown, he will head to the St. Louis University

School of Medicine. At the Christian Union conference in 2005, he was pleased to hear doctors talk about praying with their patients and traveling as medical missionaries.

He is looking forward to having the money a medical degree can bring, and especially to putting his children through college without the scholarships and part-time jobs he needed. But whether he becomes rich, he said, "will depend on how much I keep."

Like other evangelicals of his generation, he means to take his faith with him as he makes his way in the world. He said his roommates at Brown had always predicted that he would "sell out"—loosen up about his faith and adopt their taste for new cars, new clothes, and the other trappings of the upper class.

He didn't at Brown and he thinks he never will.

"So far so good," he said. But he admitted, "I don't have any money yet."

6. The College Dropout Boom

David Leonhardt

Andy Blevins, shopping with his wife, Karla, and son, Lucas, is considering going back to college, which he left in 1995. (Ting-Li Wang/*The New York Times*)

One of the biggest decisions Andy Blevins has ever made, and one of the few he now regrets, never seemed like much of a decision at all. It just felt like the natural thing to do.

In the summer of 1995, he was moving boxes of soup cans, paper towels, and dog food across the floor of a supermarket warehouse, one of the biggest buildings in the area of southwest Virginia surrounding the town of Chilhowie. The heat was brutal. The job had sounded impossible when he arrived fresh off his first year of college, looking to make some summer money, still a skinny teenager with sandy blond hair and a narrow, freckled face.

But hard work done well was something he understood, even if he was the first college boy in his family. Soon he was making bonuses on top of his $6.75 an hour, more money than either of his parents made. His girlfriend was around, and so were his hometown buddies. Andy acted more outgoing with them, more relaxed. People in Chilhowie noticed that.

It was just about the perfect summer. So the thought crossed his mind: maybe it did not have to end. Maybe he would take a break from college and keep working. He had been getting Cs and Ds, and college never felt like home, anyway.

"I enjoyed working hard, getting the job done, getting a paycheck," Blevins recalled. "I just knew I didn't want to quit."

So he quit college instead, and with that, Andy Blevins joined one of the largest and fastest-growing groups of young adults in America. He became a college dropout, though nongraduate may be the more precise term.

Many people like him plan to return to get their degrees, even if few actually do. Almost one in three Americans in their mid-twenties now fall into this group, up from one in five in the late 1960s, when the Census Bureau began keeping such data. Most come from poor and working-class families.

The phenomenon has been largely overlooked in the

glare of positive news about the country's gains in education. Going to college has become the norm throughout most of the United States, even in many places where college was once considered an exotic destination—places like Chilhowie, an Appalachian hamlet with a simple brick downtown. At elite universities, classrooms are filled with women, blacks, Jews, and Latinos, groups largely excluded two generations ago. The American system of higher learning seems to have become a great equalizer.

In fact, though, colleges have come to reinforce many of the advantages of birth. On campuses that enroll poorer students, graduation rates are often low. And at institutions where nearly everyone graduates—small colleges like Colgate, major state institutions like the University of Colorado, and elite private universities like Stanford—more students today come from the top of the nation's income ladder than they did two decades ago.

Only 41 percent of low-income students entering a four-year college managed to graduate within five years, the U.S. Department of Education found in a 2004 study, but 66 percent of high-income students did. That gap had grown over recent years.

"We need to recognize that the most serious domestic problem in the United States today is the widening gap between the children of the rich and the children of the poor," Lawrence H. Summers, the president of Harvard, said when announcing in 2004 that Harvard would give full scholarships to all its lowest-income students. "And education is the most powerful weapon we have to address that problem."

There is certainly much to celebrate about higher education today. Many more students from all classes are getting four-year degrees and reaping their benefits. But those broad gains mask the fact that poor and working-class students have nevertheless been falling behind; for them, not having a degree remains the norm.

That loss of ground is all the more significant because a college education matters much more now than it once did. A bachelor's degree, not a year or two of courses, tends to determine a person's place in today's globalized, computerized economy. College graduates have received steady pay increases over the past two decades, while the pay of everyone else has risen little more than the rate of inflation.

As a result, despite one of the great education explosions in modern history, economic mobility—moving from one income group to another over the course of a lifetime—has stopped rising, researchers say. Some recent studies suggest that it has declined over the last generation.

Put another way, children seem to be following the paths of their parents more than they once did. Grades and test scores, rather than privilege, determine success today, but that success is largely being passed down from one generation to the next. A nation that believes that everyone should have a fair shake finds itself with a kind of inherited meritocracy.

In this system, the students at the best colleges may be diverse—male and female and of various colors, religions, and hometowns—but they tend to share an upper-middle-class upbringing. An old joke that Harvard's idea of diversity is putting a rich kid from California in the same room as a rich kid from New York is truer today than ever; Harvard has more students from California than it did in years past and just as big a share of upper-income students.

Students like these remain in college because they can hardly imagine doing otherwise. Their parents, understanding the importance of a bachelor's degree, spent hours reading to them, researching school districts, and making it clear to them that they simply must graduate from college.

Andy Blevins says that he too knows the importance of a degree, but that he did not while growing up, and not even in his year at Radford University, sixty-six miles up the interstate from Chilhowie. Ten years after trading college for the warehouse, Blevins, who is twenty-nine, spends his days at the same supermarket company. He has worked his way up to produce buyer, earning $35,000 a year with health benefits and a 401(k) plan. He is on a path typical for someone who attended college without getting a four-year degree. Men in their early forties in this category made an average of $42,000 in 2000. Those with a four-year degree made $65,000.

Still boyish-looking but no longer rail thin, Blevins says he has many reasons to be happy. He lives with his wife, Karla, and their son, Lucas, in a small blue-and-yellow house at the end of a cul-de-sac in the middle of a stunningly picturesque Appalachian valley. He plays golf with some of the same friends who made him want to stay around Chilhowie.

But he does think about what might have been, about what he could be doing if he had the degree. As it is, he always feels as if he is on thin ice. Were he to lose his job, he says, everything could slip away with it. What kind of job could a guy without a college degree get? One night, while talking to his wife about his life, he used the word "trapped."

"Looking back, I wish I had gotten that degree," Blevins said in his soft-spoken lilt. "Four years seemed like a thousand years then. But I wish I would have just put in my four years."

THE BARRIERS

Why so many low-income students fall from the college ranks is a question without a simple answer. Many high schools do a poor job of preparing teenagers for college. Many of the colleges where lower-income students tend to enroll have limited resources and offer a narrow range of majors, leaving some students disenchanted and unwilling to continue.

Then there is the cost. Tuition bills scare some students from even applying and leave others with years of debt. To Blevins, like many other students of limited means, every week of going to classes seemed like another week of losing money—money that might have been made at a job.

"The system makes a false promise to students," said John T. Casteen III, the president of the University of Virginia, himself the son of a Virginia shipyard worker.

Colleges, Casteen said, present themselves as meritocracies in which academic ability and hard work are always rewarded. In fact, he said, many working-class students face obstacles they cannot overcome on their own.

For much of his fifteen years as Virginia's president,

Casteen has focused on raising money and expanding the university, the most prestigious in the state. In the meantime, students with backgrounds like his have become ever scarcer on campus. The university's genteel nickname, the Cavaliers, and its aristocratic sword-crossed coat of arms seem appropriate today. No flagship state university has a smaller proportion of low-income students than Virginia. Just 8 percent of undergraduates in 2004 came from families in the bottom half of the income distribution, down from 11 percent a decade earlier.

That change sneaked up on him, Casteen said, and he had spent a good part of the previous year trying to prevent it from becoming part of his legacy. Starting with the fall 2005 freshman class, the university will charge no tuition and require no loans for students whose parents make less than twice the poverty level, or about $37,700 a year for a family of four. The university has also increased financial aid to middle-income students.

To Casteen, these are steps to remove what he describes as "artificial barriers" to a college education placed in the way of otherwise deserving students. Doing so "is a fundamental obligation of a free culture," he said.

But the deterrents to a degree can also be homegrown. Many low-income teenagers know few people who have made it through college. A majority of the nongraduates are young men, and some come from towns where the factory work ethic, to get working as soon as possible, remains strong, even if the factories themselves are vanishing. Whatever the reasons, college just does not feel normal.

—

"You get there and you start to struggle," said Leanna Blevins, Andy's older sister, who did get a bachelor's degree and then went on to earn a Ph.D. at Virginia studying the college experiences of poor students. "And at home your parents are trying to be supportive and say, 'Well, if you're not happy, if it's not right for you, come back home. It's okay.' And they think they're doing the right thing. But they don't know that maybe what the student needs is to hear them say, 'Stick it out just one semester. You can do it. Just stay there. Come home on the weekend, but stick it out.'"

Today, Leanna, petite and high-energy, is helping to start a new college a few hours' drive from Chilhowie for low-income students. Her brother said he had daydreamed about attending it and had talked to her about how he might return to college.

For her part, Leanna says, she has daydreamed about having a life that would seem as natural as her brother's, a life in which she would not feel like an outsider in her hometown. Once, when a high school teacher asked students to list their goals for the next decade, she wrote, "having a college degree" and "not being married."

"I think my family probably thinks I'm liberal," Leanna, who is now married, said with a laugh, "that I've just been educated too much and I'm gettin' above my raisin'."

Her brother said that he just wanted more control over his life, not a new one. At a time when many people complain of scattered lives, Andy Blevins can stand in one spot—his church parking lot, next to a graveyard—and take in much of his world. "That's my parents' house," he said one day, pointing to a sliver of roof visible over a hill. "That's my uncle's trailer. My grandfather is buried here. I'll probably be buried here."

TAKING CLASS INTO ACCOUNT

Opening up colleges to new kinds of students has generally meant one thing over the last generation: affirmative action. Intended to right the wrongs of years of exclusion, the programs have swelled the number of women, blacks, and Latinos on campuses. But affirmative action was never supposed to address broad economic inequities, just the ones that stem from specific kinds of discrimination.

That is now beginning to change. Like Virginia, a handful of other colleges are not only increasing financial aid but also promising to give weight to economic class in granting admissions. They say they want to make an effort to admit more low-income students, just as they now do for minorities and children of alumni.

"The great colleges and universities were designed to provide for mobility, to seek out talent," said Anthony W. Marx, president of Amherst College. "If we are blind to the educational disadvantages associated with need, we will simply replicate these disadvantages while appearing to make decisions based on merit."

With several populous states having already banned race-based preferences and the United States Supreme Court suggesting that it may outlaw such programs in a couple of decades, the future of affirmative action may well revolve around economics. Polls consistently show that programs based on class backgrounds have wider support than those based on race.

The explosion in the number of nongraduates has also begun to get the attention of policy makers. In 2005, New York became one of a small group of states to tie college financing more closely to graduation rates, rewarding colleges more for moving students along than for simply admitting them. Nowhere is the stratification of education more vivid than in Virginia, where Thomas Jefferson once tried, and failed, to set up the nation's first public high schools. At a modest high school in the Tidewater city of Portsmouth, not far from John Casteen's boyhood home, a guidance-office wall filled with college pennants does not include one from rarefied Virginia. The colleges whose pennants are up—Old Dominion University and others that seem in the realm of the possible—have far lower graduation rates.

Across the country, the upper middle class so dominates elite universities that high-income students, on average, actually get slightly more financial aid from colleges than low-income students do. These elite colleges are so expensive that even many high-income students receive large grants. In the early 1990s, by contrast, poorer students got 50 percent more aid on average than the wealthier ones, according to the College Board, the organization that runs the SAT entrance exams.

At the other end of the spectrum are community colleges, the two-year institutions that are intended to be feeders for four-year colleges. In nearly every one are tales of academic success against tremendous odds: a battered wife or a combat veteran or a laid-off worker on the way to a better life. But overall, community colleges tend to be places where dreams are put on hold.

Most people who enroll say they plan to get a four-year degree eventually; few actually do. Full-time jobs, commutes, and children or parents who need care often get in the way. One recent national survey found that about 75 percent of students enrolling in community colleges said they hoped to transfer to a four-year institution. But only 17 percent of those who had entered in the mid-1990s made the switch within five years, according to a separate study. The rest were out working or still studying toward the two-year degree.

"We here in Virginia do a good job of getting them in," said Glenn Dubois, chancellor of the Virginia Community College System and himself a community college graduate. "We have to get better in getting them out."

"I WEAR A TIE EVERY DAY"

College degree or not, Andy Blevins has the kind of life that many Americans say they aspire to. He fills it with family, friends, church, and a five-handicap golf game. He does not sit in traffic commuting to an office park. He does not talk wistfully of a relocated brother or best friend he sees only twice a year. He does not worry about who will care for his son while he works and his wife attends community college to become a physical therapist. His grandparents down the street watch Lucas, just as they took care of Andy and his two sisters when they were children. When he comes home from work, it is his turn to play with Lucas, tossing him into the air and rolling around on the floor with him and a stuffed elephant.

Blevins also sings in a quartet called the Gospel Gentlemen. One member is his brother-in-law; another lives on his street. In the long white van the group owns, they wend their way along mountain roads on their way to singing dates at local church functions, sometimes harmonizing, sometimes ribbing one another or talking about where to buy golf equipment.

Inside the churches, the other singers often talk to the audience between songs, about God or a grandmother or what a song means to them. Blevins rarely does, but his shyness fades once he is back in the van with his friends.

At the warehouse, he is usually the first to arrive, around 6:30 in the morning. The grandson of a coal miner, he takes pride, he says, in having moved up to become a supermarket buyer. He decides which bananas, grapes, onions, and potatoes the company will sell and makes sure that there is always enough. Most people with his job have graduated from college.

"I'm pretty fortunate to not have a degree but have a job where I wear a tie every day," he said.

He worries about how long it will last, though, mindful of what happened to his father, Dwight, a decade ago. A high school graduate, Dwight Blevins was laid off from his own warehouse job and ended up with another one that paid less and offered a smaller pension.

"A lot of places, they're not looking that you're trained in something," Andy Blevins said one evening, sitting on his back porch. "They just want you to have a degree."

Figuring out how to get one is the core quandary facing the nation's college nongraduates. Many seem to want one. In a *New York Times* poll, 43 percent of them called it essential to success, while 42 percent of college graduates and 32 percent of high school dropouts did. This in itself is a change from the days when "college boy" was an insult in many working-class neighborhoods. But once students take a break—the phrase that many use instead of "drop out"—the ideal can quickly give way to reality. Family and work can make a return to school seem even harder than finishing it in the first place.

After dropping out of Radford, Andy Blevins enrolled part-time in a community college, trying to juggle work and studies. He lasted a year. From time to time in the decade since, he has thought about giving it another try. But then he has wondered if that would be crazy. He works every third Saturday, and his phone rings on Sundays when there is a problem with the supply of potatoes or apples. "It never ends," he said. "There's never a lull."

To spend more time with Lucas, Blevins has already cut back on his singing. If he took night classes, he said, when would he ever see his little boy? Anyway, he said, it would take years to get a degree part-time. To him, it is a tug-of-war between living in the present and sacrificing for the future.

—

FEW BREAKS FOR THE NEEDY

The college admissions system often seems ruthlessly meritocratic. Yes, children of alumni still have an advantage. But many other pillars of the old system—the polite rejections of women or blacks, the spots reserved for graduates of Choate and Exeter—have crumbled.

This was the meritocracy John Casteen described when he greeted the parents of freshmen in a University of Virginia lecture hall in the late summer of 2004. Hailing from all fifty states and fifty-two foreign countries, the students were more intelligent and better prepared than he and his classmates had been, he told the parents in his quiet, deep voice. The class included seventeen students with a perfect SAT score.

If anything, children of privilege think that the system has moved so far from its old-boy history that they are now at a disadvantage when they apply, because colleges are trying to diversify their student rolls. To get into a good college, the sons and daughters of the upper middle class often talk of needing a higher SAT score than, say, an applicant who grew up on a farm, in a ghetto, or in a factory town. Some state legislators from northern Virginia's affluent suburbs have argued that this is a form of geographic discrimination and have quixotically proposed bills to outlaw it.

But the conventional wisdom is not quite right. The elite colleges have not been giving much of a break to the low-income students who apply. When William G. Bowen, a former president of Princeton, looked at admissions records recently, he found that if test scores were equal a low-income student had no better chance than a high-income one of getting into a group of nineteen colleges, including Harvard, Yale, Princeton, Williams, and Virginia. Athletes, legacy applicants, and minority students all got in with lower scores on average. Poorer students did not.

The findings befuddled many administrators, who insist that admissions officers have tried to give poorer applicants a leg up. To emphasize the point, Virginia announced in the spring of 2005 that it was changing its admissions policy from "need blind"—a term long used to assure applicants that they would not be punished for seeking financial aid—to "need conscious." Administrators at Amherst and Harvard have also recently said that they would redouble their efforts to take into account the obstacles students have overcome.

"The same score reflects more ability when you come from a less fortunate background," Lawrence Summers, the president of Harvard, said. "You haven't had a chance to take the test-prep course. You went to a school that didn't do as good a job coaching you for the test. You came from a home without the same opportunities for learning."

But it is probably not a coincidence that elite colleges have not yet turned this sentiment into action. Admitting large numbers of low-income students could bring clear complications. Too many in a freshman class would probably lower the college's average SAT score, thereby damaging its ranking by *U.S. News & World Report*, a leading arbiter of academic prestige. Some colleges, like Emory University in Atlanta, have climbed fast in the rankings over precisely the same period in which their percentage of low-income students has tumbled. The math is simple: when a college goes looking for applicants with high SAT scores, it is far more likely to find them among well-off teenagers.

More spots for low-income applicants might also mean fewer for the children of alumni, who make up the fundraising base for universities. More generous financial aid policies will probably lead to higher tuition for those students who can afford the list price. Higher tuition, lower ranking, tougher admission requirements: these do not make for an easy marketing pitch to alumni clubs around the country. But Casteen and his colleagues are going ahead, saying the pendulum has swung too far in one direction.

That was the mission of John Blackburn, Virginia's easygoing admissions dean, when he rented a car and took to the road in the spring of 2005. Blackburn thought of the trip as a reprise of the drives Casteen took twenty-five years earlier, when he was the admissions dean, traveling to churches and community centers to persuade black parents that the university was finally interested in their children.

One Monday night, Blackburn came to Big Stone Gap, in a mostly poor corner of the state not far from Andy Blevins's town. A community college there was holding a college fair, and Blackburn set up a table in a hallway, draping it with the University of Virginia's blue and orange flag.

As students came by, Blackburn would explain Virginia's new admissions and financial aid policies. But he soon realized that the Virginia name might have been scaring off the very people his pitch was intended for. Most of the students

who did approach the table showed little interest in the financial aid and expressed little need for it. One man walked up to Blackburn and introduced his son as an aspiring doctor. The father was an ophthalmologist. Other doctors came by, too. So did some lawyers.

"You can't just raise the UVA flag," Blackburn said, packing up his materials at the end of the night, "and expect a lot of low-income kids to come out."

When the applications started arriving in his office, there seemed to be no increase in those from low-income students. So Blackburn extended the deadline two weeks for everybody, and his colleagues also helped some applicants with the maze of financial aid forms. Of 3,100 incoming freshmen, it now seems that about 180 will qualify for the new financial aid program, up from 130 who would have done so the year before. It is not a huge number, but Virginia administrators call it a start.

A BIG DECISION

On a still-dark February morning, with the winter's heaviest snowfall on the ground, Andy Blevins scraped off his Jeep and began his daily drive to the supermarket warehouse. As he passed the home of Mike Nash, his neighbor and fellow gospel singer, he noticed that the car was still in the driveway. For Nash, a school counselor and the only college graduate in the singing group, this was a snow day.

Blevins later sat down with his calendar and counted to 280: the number of days he had worked last year. Two hundred

and eighty days—six days a week most of the time—without ever really knowing what the future would hold.

"I just realized I'm going to have to do something about this," he said, "because it's never going to end."

In the weeks afterward, his daydreaming about college and his conversations about it with his sister Leanna turned into serious research. He requested his transcripts from Radford and from Virginia Highlands Community College and figured out that he had about a year's worth of credits. He also talked to Leanna about how he could become an elementary school teacher. He always felt that he could relate to children, he said. The job would take up 180 days, not 280. Teachers do not usually get laid off or lose their pensions or have to take a big pay cut to find new work.

So the decision was made. Andy Blevins says he will return to Virginia Highlands, taking classes at night; the Gospel Gentlemen are no longer booking performances. After a year, he plans to take classes by video and on the Web that are offered at the community college but run by Old Dominion, a Norfolk, Virginia, university with a big group of working-class students.

"I don't like classes, but I've gotten so motivated to go back to school," Blevins said. "I don't want to, but, then again, I do."

He thinks he can get his bachelor's degree in three years. If he gets it at all, he will have defied the odds.

7. No Degree, and No Way Back to the Middle

Timothy Egan

Jeff Martinelli began working in pest control after he lost a job that had established him in the middle class. (Jim Wilson/*The New York Times*)

Over the course of his adult life, Jeff Martinelli has married three women and buried one of them, a cancer victim. He had a son and has watched him raise a child of his own. Through it all, one thing was constant: a factory job that was his ticket to the middle class.

It was not until that job disappeared, and he tried to find

something—anything—to keep him close to the security of his former life that Martinelli came to an abrupt realization about the fate of a workingman with no college degree in twenty-first-century America.

He has skills developed operating heavy machinery, laboring over a stew of molten bauxite at Kaiser Aluminum, once one of the best jobs in Spokane, Washington, a city of 200,000. His health is fine. He has no shortage of ambition. But the world has changed for people like him.

"For a guy like me, with no college, it's become pretty bleak out there," said Martinelli, who is fifty years old and deals with life's curves with a resigned shrug.

His son Caleb already knows what it is like out there. Since high school, Caleb has had six jobs, none very promising. Now twenty-eight, he may never reach the middle class, he said. But for his father and others of a generation that could count on a comfortable life without a degree, the fall out of the middle class has come as a shock. They had been frozen in another age, a time when Kaiser factory workers could buy new cars, take decent vacations, and enjoy full health care benefits.

They have seen factory gates close and not reopen. They have taken retraining classes for jobs that pay half their old wages. And as they hustle around for work, they have been constantly reminded of the one thing that stands out on their résumés: the education that ended with a high school diploma.

It is not just that the American economy has shed six million manufacturing jobs over the last three decades; it is that the market value of those put out of work, people like Jeff Martinelli, has declined considerably over their lifetimes, opening a gap that has left millions of blue-collar workers at the margins of the middle class.

And the changes go beyond the factory floor. Mark McClellan worked his way up from the Kaiser furnaces to management. He did it by taking extra shifts and learning everything he could about the aluminum business.

Still, in 2001, when Kaiser closed, McClellan discovered that the job market did not value his factory skills nearly as much as it did four years of college. He had the experience, built over a lifetime, but no degree. And for that, he said, he was marked.

He still lives in a grand house in one of the nicest parts of town, and he drives a big white Jeep. But they are a facade.

"I may look middle class," said McClellan, who is forty-five, with a square, honest face and a barrel chest. "But I'm not. My boat is sinking fast."

By the time these two Kaiser men were forced out of work, a man in his fifties with a college degree could expect to earn 81 percent more than a man of the same age with just a high school diploma. When they started work, the gap was only 52 percent. Other studies show different numbers, but the same trend—a big disparity that opened over their lifetimes.

Martinelli refuses to feel sorry for himself. He has a job in pest control now, killing ants and spiders at people's homes, making barely half the money he made at the Kaiser smelter, where a worker with his experience would make about $60,000 a year in wages and benefits.

"At least I have a job," he said. "Some of the guys I worked with have still not found anything. A couple of guys lost their houses."

Martinelli and other former factory workers say that, over time, they have come to fear that the fall out of the middle class could be permanent. Their new lives—the frustrating job interviews, the bills that arrive with red warning letters on the outside—are consequences of a decision made at age eighteen.

The management veteran McClellan was a doctor's son, just out of high school, when he decided he did not need to go much farther than the big factory at the edge of town. He thought about going to college. But when he got on at Kaiser, he felt he had arrived.

His father, a general practitioner, now dead, gave him his blessing, even encouraged him in the choice, McClellan said.

At the time, the decision to skip college was not that unusual, even for a child of the middle class. Despite McClellan's lack of skills or education beyond the twelfth grade, there was good reason to believe that the aluminum factory could get him into middle-class security quicker than a bachelor's degree could, he said.

By twenty-two, he was a group foreman. By twenty-eight, a supervisor. By thirty-two, he was in management. Before his fortieth birthday, McClellan hit his earnings peak, making $100,000 with bonuses.

Friends of his, people with college degrees, were not earning close to that, he said.

"I had a house with a swimming pool, new cars," he said. "My wife never had to work. I was right in the middle of middle-class America and I knew it and I loved it."

If anything, the union man, Martinelli, appreciated the middle-class life even more, because of the distance he had traveled to get there. He remembers his stomach growling at night as a child, the humiliation of welfare, hauling groceries home through the snow on a little cart because the family had no car.

"I was ashamed," he said.

He was a C student without much of a future, just out of high school, when he got his break: the job on the Kaiser factory floor. Inside, it was long shifts around hot furnaces. Outside, he was a prince of Spokane.

College students worked inside the factory in the summer, and some never went back to school.

"You knew people leaving here for college would sometimes get better jobs, but you had a good job, so it was fine," said Mike Lacy, a close friend of Martinelli and a coworker at Kaiser.

The job lasted just short of thirty years. Kaiser, debt-ridden after a series of failed management initiatives and a long strike, closed the plant in 2001 and sold the factory carcass for salvage.

McClellan has yet to find work, living off his dwindling savings and investments from his years at Kaiser, though he continues with plans to open his own car wash. He pays $900 a month for a basic health insurance policy—vital to keep his wife, Vicky, who has a rare brain disease, alive. He pays an additional $500 a month for her medications. He is both husband and nurse.

"Am I scared just a little bit?" he said. "Yeah, I am."

He has vowed that his son David will never do the kind of second-guessing that he does. Even at sixteen, David knows what he wants to do: go to college and study medicine. He said his father, whom he has seen struggle to balance the tasks of home nurse with trying to pay the bills, had grown heroic in his eyes.

He said he would not make the same choice his father did twenty-seven years earlier. "There's nothing like the Kaiser plant around here anymore," he said.

McClellan agrees. He is firm in one conclusion, having risen from the factory floor only to be knocked down: "There is no working up anymore."

8. Fifteen Years on the Bottom Rung

Anthony DePalma

Juan Manuel Peralta has worked kitchen jobs in New York City since he came to the United States in 1990. (Angel Franco/*The New York Times*)

In the dark before dawn, when Madison Avenue was all but deserted and its pricey boutiques were still locked up tight, several Mexicans slipped quietly into 3 Guys, a restaurant that the Zagat guide once called "the most expensive coffee shop in New York."

For the next ten hours they would fry eggs, grill burgers, pour coffee, and wash dishes for a stream of customers from

the Upper East Side of Manhattan. By 7:35 a.m., Eliot
Spitzer, attorney general of New York, was holding a power
breakfast back near the polished granite counter. In the same
burgundy booth a few hours later, Michael A. Wiener,
cofounder of the multibillion-dollar Infinity Broadcasting,
grabbed a bite with his wife, Zena. Just the day before, Uma
Thurman slipped in for a quiet lunch with her children, but
the paparazzi found her and she left.

More Mexicans filed in to begin their shifts throughout
the morning, and by the time John Zannikos, one of the
restaurant's three Greek owners, drove in from the north
Jersey suburbs to work the lunch crowd, Madison Avenue
was buzzing. So was 3 Guys.

"You got to wait a little bit," Zannikos said to a pride of
elegant women who had spent the morning at the Whitney
Museum of American Art, across Madison Avenue at 75th
Street. For an illiterate immigrant who came to New York
years ago with nothing but $100 in his pocket and a willing-
ness to work etched on his heart, could any words have been
sweeter to say?

With its wealthy clientele, middle-class owners, and
low-income workforce, 3 Guys is a template of the class divisions in America. But it is also the setting for two starkly different tales about breaching those divides.

The familiar story is Zannikos's. For him, the restaurant—
don't dare call it a diner—with its twenty-dollar salads and
elegant décor represents the American promise of upward
mobility, one that has been fulfilled countless times for generations of hardworking immigrants.

But for Juan Manuel Peralta, a thirty-four-year-old illegal immigrant who worked there for five years until he was fired in May 2004, and for many of the other illegal Mexican immigrants in the back, restaurant work today is more like a dead end. They are finding the American dream of moving up far more elusive than it was for Zannikos. Despite his efforts to help them, they risk becoming stuck in a permanent underclass of the poor, the unskilled, and the uneducated.

That is not to suggest that the nearly five million Mexicans who, like Peralta, are living in the United States illegally will never emerge from the shadows. Many have, and undoubtedly many more will. But the sheer size of the influx—over 400,000 a year, with no end in sight—creates a problem all its own. It means there is an ever-growing pool of interchangeable workers, many of them shunting from one low-paying job to another. If one moves on, another one—or maybe two or three—is there to take his place.

Although Peralta arrived in New York almost forty years after Zannikos, the two share a remarkably similar beginning. They came at the same age to the same section of New York City, without legal papers or more than a few words of English. Each dreamed of a better life. But monumental changes in the economy and in attitudes toward immigrants have made it far less likely that Peralta and his children will experience the same upward mobility as Zannikos and his family.

Of course, there is a chance that Peralta may yet take his place among the Mexican-Americans who have succeeded here. He realizes that he will probably not do as well as the few who have risen to high office or who were able to buy the vineyards where their grandfathers once picked grapes. But he still dreams that his children will someday join the millions who have lost their accents, gotten good educations, and firmly achieved the American dream.

Political scientists are divided over whether the twenty-five million people of Mexican ancestry in the United States represent an exception to the classic immigrant success story. Some, like John H. Mollenkopf at the City University of New York, are convinced that Mexicans will eventually do as well as the Greeks, Italians, and other Europeans of the last century who were usually well assimilated after two or three generations. Others, including Mexican-Americans like Rodolfo O. de la Garza, a professor at Columbia, have done studies showing that Mexican-Americans face so many obstacles that even the fourth generation trails other Americans in education, home ownership, and household income.

The situation is even worse for the millions more who have illegally entered the United States since 1990. Spread out in scores of cities far beyond the Southwest, they find jobs plentiful but advancement difficult. President Vicente Fox of Mexico was forced to apologize in the spring of 2005 for declaring publicly what many Mexicans say they feel, that the illegal immigrants "are doing the work that not even blacks want to do in the United States." Resentment and race subtly stand in their way, as does a lingering attachment to Mexico, which is so close that many immigrants do not put down deep roots here. They say they plan to stay only long enough to make some money and then go back home. Few ever do.

But the biggest obstacle is their illegal status. With few routes open to become legal, they remain, like Peralta, without rights, without security, and without a clear path to a better future.

"It's worrisome," said Richard Alba, a sociologist at the State University of New York, Albany, who studies the assimilation and class mobility of contemporary immigrants, "and I don't see much reason to believe this will change."

Little has changed for Peralta, a cook who has worked at menial jobs in the United States for fifteen years. Though he makes more than he ever dreamed of in Mexico, his life is anything but middle class and setbacks are routine. Still, he has not given up hope. *"Querer es poder,"* he sometimes says—want something badly enough and you will get it.

But desire may not be enough anymore. That is what concerns Arturo Sarukhan, Mexico's consul general in New York. In early 2005, Sarukhan took an urgent call from New York's police commissioner about an increase in gang activity among young Mexican men, a sign that they were moving into the underside of American life. Of all immigrants in New York City, officials say, Mexicans are the poorest, least educated, and least likely to speak English.

The failure or success of this generation of Mexicans in the United States will determine the place that Mexicans will hold here in years to come, Sarukhan said, and the outlook is not encouraging.

"They will be better off than they could ever have been in Mexico," he said, "but I don't think that's going to be enough to prevent them from becoming an underclass in New York."

DIFFERENT RESULTS

There is a break in the middle of the day at 3 Guys, after the lunchtime limousines leave and before the private schools let out. That was when Zannikos asked the Mexican cook who replaced Peralta to prepare some lunch for him. Then Zannikos carried the chicken breast on pita to the last table in the restaurant.

"My life story is a good story, a lot of success," he said, his accent still heavy. He was just a teenager when he left the Greek island of Chios, a few miles off the coast of Turkey. World War II had just ended, and Greece was in ruins. "There was only rich and poor, that's it," Zannikos said. "There was no middle class like you have here." He is seventy now, with short gray hair and soft eyes that can water at a mention of the past.

Because of the war, he said, he never got past the second grade, never learned to read or write. He signed on as a merchant seaman, and in 1953, when he was nineteen, his ship docked at Norfolk, Virginia. He went ashore one Saturday with no intention of ever returning to Greece. He left behind everything, including his travel documents. All he had in his pockets was $100 and the address of his mother's cousin in the Jackson Heights–Corona section of Queens.

Almost four decades later, Juan Manuel Peralta underwent a similar rite of passage out of Mexico. He had finished the eighth grade in the poor southern state of Guerrero and saw nothing in his future there but fixing flat tires. His father, Inocencio, had once dreamed of going to the United States, but never had the money. In 1990, he borrowed enough to give his firstborn son a chance.

Peralta was nineteen when he boarded a smoky bus that carried him through the deserted hills of Guerrero and kept going until it reached the edge of Mexico. With eight other Mexicans he did not know, he crawled through a sewer tunnel that started in Tijuana and ended on the other side of the border, in what Mexicans call El Norte.

He had carried no documents, no photographs, and no money except what his father gave him to pay his shifty guide and to buy an airline ticket to New York. Deep in a pocket was the address of an uncle in the same section of Queens where John Zannikos had gotten his start. By 1990, the area had gone from largely Greek to mostly Latino.

Starting over in the same working-class neighborhood, Peralta and Zannikos quickly learned that New York was full of opportunities and obstacles, often in equal measure. On his first day there, Zannikos, scared and feeling lost, found the building he was looking for, but his mother's cousin had moved. He had no idea what to do until a Greek man passed by. Walk five blocks to the Deluxe Diner, the man said. He did.

The diner was full of Greek housepainters, including one who knew Zannikos's father. On the spot, they offered him a job painting closets, where his mistakes would be hidden. He painted until the weather turned cold. Another

Greek hired him as a dishwasher at his coffee shop in the Bronx.

It was not easy, but Zannikos worked his way up to short-order cook, learning English as he went along. In 1956, immigration officials raided the coffee shop. He was deported, but after a short while he managed to sneak back into the country. Three years later he married a Puerto Rican from the Bronx. The marriage lasted only a year, but it put him on the road to becoming a citizen. Now he could buy his own restaurant, a greasy spoon in the South Bronx that catered to a late-night clientele of prostitutes and undercover police officers.

Since then, he has bought and sold more than a dozen New York diners, but none have been more successful than the original 3 Guys, which opened in 1978. He and his partners own two other restaurants with the same name farther up Madison Avenue, but they have never replicated the high-end appeal of the original.

"When employees come in, I teach them, 'Hey, this is a different neighborhood,'" Zannikos said. What may be standard in some other diners is not tolerated here. There are no Greek flags or tourism posters. There is no television or twirling tower of cakes with cream pompadours. Waiters are forbidden to chew gum. No customer is ever called "Honey."

"They know their place and I know my place," Zannikos said of his customers. "It's as simple as that."

His place in society now is a far cry from his days in the Bronx. He and his second wife, June, live in Wyckoff, a New Jersey suburb where he pampers fig trees and dutifully looks after a bird feeder shaped like the Parthenon. They own a condominium in Florida. His three children all went far beyond his second-grade education, finishing high school or attending college.

They have all done well, as has Zannikos, who says he makes about $130,000 a year. He says he is not sensitive to class distinctions, but he admits he was bothered when some people mistook him for the caterer at fund-raising dinners for the local Greek church he helped build.

All in all, he thinks immigrants today have a better chance of moving up the class ladder than he did fifty years ago.

"At that time, no bank would give us any money, but today they give you credit cards in the mail," he said. "New York still gives you more opportunity than any other place. If you want to do things, you will."

He says he has done well, and he is content with his station in life. "I'm in the middle and I'm happy."

A DIVISIVE ISSUE

Juan Manuel Peralta cannot guess what class John Zannikos belongs to. But he is certain that it is much tougher for an immigrant to get ahead today than fifty years ago. And he has no doubt about his own class.

"*La pobreza*," he says. "Poverty."

It was not what he expected when he boarded the bus to the border, but it did not take long for him to realize that success in the United States required more than hard work. "A lot of it has to do with luck," he said during a lunch break on a stoop around the corner from the Queens diner where he went to work after 3 Guys.

"People come here, and in no more than a year or two they can buy their own house and have a car," Peralta said. "Me, I've been here fifteen years, and if I die tomorrow, there wouldn't even be enough money to bury me."

In 1990, Peralta was in the vanguard of Mexican immigrants who bypassed the traditional barrios in border states to work in far-flung cities like Denver and New York. The 2000 census counted 186,872 Mexicans in New York, triple the 1990 figure, and there are undoubtedly many more today. The Mexican consulate, which serves the metropolitan region, has issued more than 500,000 ID cards just since 2001.

Fifty years ago, illegal immigration was a minor problem. Now it is a divisive national issue, pitting those who welcome cheap labor against those with concerns about border security and the cost of providing social services. Though newly arrived Mexicans often work in industries that rely on cheap labor, like restaurants and construction, they rarely organize. Most are desperate to stay out of sight.

Peralta hooked up with his uncle the morning he arrived in New York. He did not work for weeks until the bakery where the uncle worked had an opening, a part-time job making muffins. He took it, though he didn't know muffins from crumb cake. When he saw that he would not make enough to repay his father, he took a second job making night deliveries for a Manhattan diner. By the end of his first day he was so lost he had to spend all his tip money on a cab ride home.

He quit the diner, but working there even briefly opened his eyes to how easy it could be to make money in New York. Diners were everywhere, and so were jobs making deliveries, washing dishes, or busing tables. In six months, Peralta had paid back the money his father gave him. He bounced from job to job and in 1995, eager to show off his newfound success, went back to Mexico with his pockets full of money, and married. He was twenty-five then, the same age at which Zannikos married. But the similarities end there.

When Zannikos jumped ship, he left Greece behind for good. Though he himself had no documents, the compatriots he encountered on his first days were here legally, like most other Greek immigrants, and could help him. Greeks had never come to the United States in large numbers—the 2000 census counted only 29,805 New Yorkers born in Greece—but they tended to settle in just a few areas, like the Astoria section of Queens, which became cohesive communities ready to help new arrivals.

Peralta, like many other Mexicans, is trying to make it on his own and has never severed his emotional or financial ties to home. After five years in New York's Latino community, he spoke little English and owned little more than the clothes on his back. He decided to return to Huamuxtitlán, the dusty village beneath a flat-topped mountain where he was born.

"People thought that since I was coming back from El Norte, I would be so rich that I could spread money around," he said. Still, he felt privileged: his New York wages dwarfed the $1,000 a year he might have made in Mexico.

He met a shy, pretty girl named Matilde in Huamuxtitlán, married her, and returned with her to New York, again illegally, all in a matter of weeks. Their first child was born in 1996. Peralta soon found that supporting a family made it harder to save money. Then, in 1999, he got the job at 3 Guys.

"Barba Yanni helped me learn how to prepare things the way customers like them," Peralta said, referring to Zannikos with a Greek title of respect that means Uncle John.

The restaurant became his school. He learned how to sauté a fish so that it looked like a work of art. The three partners lent him money and said they would help him get immigration documents. The pay was good.

But there were tensions with the other workers. Instead of hanging their orders on a rack, the waiters shouted them out, in Greek, Spanish, and a kind of fractured English. Sometimes Peralta did not understand, and they argued. Soon he was known as a hothead.

Still, he worked hard, and every night he returned to his growing family. Matilde, now twenty-seven, cleaned houses until their second child, Heidi, was born in 2002. Now Matilde tries to sell Mary Kay products to other mothers at Public School 12, which their son Antony, who is eight, attends.

Most weeks, Peralta could make as much as $600. Over the course of a year that could come to over $30,000, enough to approach the lower middle class. But the life he leads is far from that and uncertainty hovers over everything about his life, starting with his paycheck.

To earn $600, he has to work at least ten hours a day, six

days a week, and that does not happen every week. Sometimes he is paid overtime for the extra hours, sometimes not. And, as he found out, he can be fired at any time and bring in nothing, not even unemployment, until he lands another job. In 2004, he made about $24,000.

Because he is here illegally, Peralta can easily be exploited. He cannot file a complaint against his landlord for charging him $500 a month for a nine- by nine-foot room in a Queens apartment that he shares with nine other Mexicans in three families who pay the remainder of the $2,000-a-month rent. All thirteen share one bathroom, and the established pecking order means the Peraltas rarely get to use the kitchen. Eating out can be expensive.

Because they were born in New York, Peralta's children are United States citizens, and their health care is generally covered by Medicaid. But he has to pay out of his pocket whenever he or his wife sees a doctor. And forget about going to the dentist.

As many other Mexicans do, he wires money home, and it costs him $7 for every $100 he sends. When his uncle, his nephew, and his sister asked him for money, he was expected to lend it. No one has paid him back. He has middle-class ornaments, like a cellphone and a DVD player, but no driver's license or Social Security card.

He is the first to admit that he has vices that have held him back; nothing criminal, but he tends to lose his temper and there are nights when he likes to have a drink or two. His greatest weakness is instant lottery tickets, what he calls "*los scratch*," and he sheepishly confesses that he can squander as much as $75 a week on them. It is a way of preserving hope, he said. Once he won $100. He bought a blender.

Years ago, he and Matilde were so confident they would make it in America that when their son was born they used the American spelling of his name, Anthony, figuring it would help pave his passage into the mainstream. But even that effort failed.

"Look at this," his wife said one afternoon as she sat on the floor of their room near a picture of the Virgin of Guadalupe. Peralta sat on a small plastic stool in the doorway, listening. His mattress was stacked against the wall. A roll of toilet paper was stashed nearby because they dared not leave it in the shared bathroom for someone else to use.

She took her pocketbook and pulled out a clear plastic case holding her son's baptismal certificate, on which his name is spelled with an *H*. But then she unfolded his birth certificate, where the *H* is missing.

"The teachers won't teach him to spell his name the right way until the certificate is legally changed," she said. "But how can we do that if we're not legal?"

PROGRESS, BUT NOT SUCCESS

An elevated subway train thundered overhead, making the afternoon light along Roosevelt Avenue blink like a failing fluorescent bulb. Peralta's daughter and son grabbed his fat hands as they ran some errands. He had just finished a ten-hour shift, eggs over easy and cheeseburgers since 5:00 a.m. It had been especially hard to stand the monotony that day.

He kept thinking about what was going on in Mexico, where it was the feast day of Our Lady of the Rosary. And, oh, what a feast there was—sweets and handmade tamales, a parade, even a bullfight. At night, fireworks, bursting loud and bright against the green folds of the mountains. Paid for, in part, by the money he sends home.

But instead of partying, he was walking his children to the Arab supermarket on Roosevelt Avenue to buy packages of chicken and spare ribs, and hoping to get to use the kitchen. And though he knew better, he grabbed a package of pink and white marshmallows for the children. He needed to buy tortillas, too, but not there. A Korean convenience store a few blocks away sells La Maizteca tortillas, made in New York.

The swirl of immigrants in Peralta's neighborhood is part of the fabric of New York, just as it was in 1953, when John Zannikos arrived. But most immigrants then were Europeans, and though they spoke different languages, their Caucasian features helped them blend into New York's middle class.

Experts remain divided over whether Mexicans can follow the same route. Samuel P. Huntington, a Harvard professor of government, takes the extreme view that Mexicans will not assimilate and that the separate culture they are developing threatens the United States.

Most others believe that recent Mexican immigrants will eventually take their place in society, and perhaps someday muster political clout commensurate with their numbers, though significant impediments are slowing their progress.

Francisco Rivera-Batiz, a Columbia University economics professor, says that prejudice remains a problem, that factory jobs have all but disappeared, and that there is a growing gap between the educational demands of the economy and the limited schooling that the newest Mexicans have when they arrive.

But the biggest obstacle by far, and the one that separates newly arrived Mexicans from Greeks, Italians, and most other immigrants—including earlier generations of Mexicans—is their illegal status. Rivera-Batiz studied what happened to illegal Mexican immigrants who became legal after the last national amnesty in 1986. Within a few years, their incomes rose 20 percent and their English improved greatly.

"Legalization," he said, "helped them tremendously."

Although the Bush administration talks about legalizing some Mexicans with a guest worker program, there is opposition to another amnesty, and the number of Mexicans illegally living in the United States continues to soar. Desperate to get their papers any way they can, many turn to shady storefront legal offices. Like Peralta, they sign on to illusory schemes that cost hundreds of dollars but almost never produce the promised green cards.

Until the 1980s, Mexican immigration was largely seasonal and mostly limited to agricultural workers. But then economic chaos in Mexico sent a flood of immigrants northward, many of them poorly educated farmers from the impoverished countryside. Tighter security on the border made it harder for Mexicans to move back and forth in the traditional way, so they tended to stay here, searching for low-paying unskilled jobs and concentrating in barrios where Spanish, constantly replenished, never loses its immediacy.

"*Cuidado!*" Peralta shouted when Antony carelessly stepped into Roosevelt Avenue without looking. Although the boy is taught in English at school, he rarely uses anything but Spanish at home.

Even now, after fifteen years in New York, Peralta speaks little English. He tried English classes once, but could not get his mind to accept the new sounds. So he dropped it, and has stuck with Spanish, which he concedes is "the language of busboys" in New York. But as long as he stays in his neighborhood, it is all he needs.

It was late afternoon by the time Peralta and his children headed home. The run-down house, the overheated room, the stacked mattress, and the hoarded toilet paper—all remind him how far he would have to go to achieve a success like John Zannikos's.

Still, he says, he has done far better than he could ever have done in Mexico. He realizes that the money he sends to his family there is not enough to satisfy his father, who built stairs for a second floor of his house made of concrete blocks in Huamuxtitlán, even though there is no second floor. He believes Juan Manuel has made it big in New York and he is waiting for money from America to complete the upstairs.

His son has never told him the truth about his life up north. He said his father's images of America came from another era. The older man does not know how tough it is to be a Mexican immigrant in the United States now, tougher than any young man who ever left Huamuxtitlán would admit. Everything built up over fifteen years here can come apart as easily as an adobe house in an earthquake. And then it is time to start over, again.

A CONFLICT ERUPTS

It was the end of another busy lunch at 3 Guys in the late spring of 2003. Peralta made himself a turkey sandwich and took a seat at a rear table. The Mexican countermen, dishwashers, and busboys also started their breaks, while the Greek waiters took care of the last few diners.

It is not clear how the argument started. But a cross word passed between a Greek waiter and a Mexican busboy. Voices were raised. The waiter swung at the busboy, catching him behind the ear. Peralta froze. So did the other Mexicans.

Even from the front of the restaurant, where he was watching the cash register, Zannikos realized something was wrong and rushed back to break it up. "I stood between them, held one and pushed the other away," he said. "I told them: 'You don't do that here. Never do that here.'"

Zannikos said he did not care who started it. He ordered both the busboy and the waiter, a partner's nephew, to get out.

But several Mexicans, including Peralta, said that they saw Zannikos grab the busboy by the head and that they believed he would have hit him if another Mexican had not stepped between them. That infuriated them because they felt he had sided with the Greek without knowing who was at fault.

Zannikos said that was not true, but in the end it did not matter. The easygoing atmosphere at the restaurant changed. "Everybody was a little cool," Zannikos recalled.

What he did not know then was that the Mexicans had reached out to the Restaurant Opportunities Center, a workers' rights group. Eventually six of them, including Peralta, cooperated with the group. He did so reluctantly, he said, because he was afraid that if the owners found out, they would no longer help him get his immigration papers. The labor group promised that the owners would never know.

The owners saw it as an effort to shake them down, but for the Mexicans it became a class struggle pitting powerless workers against hard-hearted owners.

Their grievances went beyond the scuffle. They complained that with just one exception, only Greeks became waiters at 3 Guys. They challenged the sole Mexican waiter, Salomon Paniagua, a former Mexican army officer who, everyone agreed, looked Greek, to stand with them.

But on the day the labor group picketed the restaurant, Paniagua refused to put down his order pad. A handful of demonstrators carried signs on Madison Avenue for a short while before Zannikos and his partners reluctantly agreed to settle.

Zannikos said he felt betrayed. "When I see these guys, I see myself when I started, and I always try to help them," he said. "I didn't do anything wrong."

The busboy and the Mexican who intervened were paid several thousand dollars and the owners promised to promote a current Mexican employee to waiter within a month. But that did not end the turmoil.

Fearing that the other Mexicans might try to get back at him, Paniagua decided to strike out on his own. After asking Zannikos for advice, he bought a one-third share of a Greek diner in Jamaica, Queens. He said he put it in his father's name because the older man had become a legal resident after the 1986 amnesty.

After Paniagua left, 3 Guys went without a single Mexican waiter for ten months, despite the terms of the settlement. In March, an eager Mexican busboy with a heavy accent who had worked there for four years got a chance to wear a waiter's tie.

Peralta ended up having to leave 3 Guys around the same time as Paniagua. Zannikos's partners suspected he had sided with the labor group, he said, and started to criticize his work unfairly. Then they cut back his schedule to five days a week. After he hurt his ankle playing soccer, they told him to go home until he was better. When Peralta came back to work about two weeks later, he was fired.

Zannikos confirms part of the account but says the firing had nothing to do with the scuffle or the ensuing dispute. "If he was good, believe me, he wouldn't get fired," he said of Peralta.

Peralta shrugged when told what Zannikos said. "I know my own work and I know what I can do," he said. "There are a lot of restaurants in New York, and a lot of workers."

When 3 Guys fired Peralta, another Mexican replaced

him, just as Peralta replaced a Mexican at the Greek diner in Queens where he went to work next.

This time, though, there was no Madison Avenue address, no elaborate menu of New Zealand mussels or designer mushrooms. In the Queens diner a bowl of soup with a buttered roll cost two dollars, all day. If he fried burgers and scraped fat off the big grill for ten hours a day, six days a week, he might earn about as much as he did on Madison Avenue, at least for a week.

His schedule kept changing. Sometimes he worked the lunch and dinner shift, and by the end of the night he was worn out, especially since he often found himself arguing with the Greek owner. But he did not look forward to going home. So after the night manager lowered the security gate, Peralta would wander the streets.

One of those nights he stopped at a phone center off Roosevelt Avenue to call his mother. "Everything's okay," he told her. He asked how she had spent the last $100 he sent, and whether she needed anything else. There is always need in Huamuxtitlán.

Still restless, he went to the Scorpion, a shot-and-beer joint open till 4 a.m. He sat at the long bar nursing vodkas with cranberry juice, glancing at the soccer match on TV and the busty Brazilian bartender who spoke only a little Spanish. When it was nearly eleven, he called it a night.

Back home, he quietly opened the door to his room. The lights were off, the television murmuring. His family was asleep in the bunk bed that the store had now threatened to repossess. Antony was curled up on the top, Matilde and Heidi cuddled in the bottom. Peralta moved the plastic stool out of the way and dropped his mattress to the floor.

The children did not stir. His wife's eyes fluttered, but she said nothing. Peralta looked over his family, his home.

"This," he said, "is my life in New York."

Not the life he imagined, but his life. In early March 2005, just after Heidi's third birthday, he quit his job at the Queens diner after yet another heated argument with the owner. In his mind, preserving his dignity is one of the few liberties he has left.

"I'll get another job," he said while babysitting Heidi at home a few days after he quit. The rent is already paid till the end of the month and he has friends, he said. People know him. To him, jobs are interchangeable—just as he is to the jobs. If he cannot find work as a grillman, he will bus tables. Or wash dishes. If not at one diner, then at another.

"It's all the same," he said.

It took about three weeks, but Peralta did find a new job as a grillman at another Greek diner in a different part of New York. His salary is roughly the same, the menu is roughly the same (one new item, Greek burritos, was a natural), and he sees his chance for a better future as being roughly the same as it has been since he got to America.

A LONG DAY CLOSES

It was now dark again outside 3 Guys. About 9:00 p.m. John Zannikos asked his Mexican cook for a small salmon steak, a little rare. It had been another busy ten-hour day for him, but a good one. Receipts from the morning alone exceeded what he needed to take in every day just to cover the $23,000 a month rent.

He finished the salmon quickly, left final instructions with the lone Greek waiter still on duty, and said good night to everyone else. He put on his light tan corduroy jacket and the baseball cap he picked up in Florida.

" 'Night," he said to the lone table of diners.

Outside, as Zannikos walked slowly down Madison Avenue, a self-made man comfortable with his own hard-won success, the bulkhead doors in front of 3 Guys clanked open. Faint voices speaking Spanish came from below. A young Mexican who started his shift ten hours earlier climbed out with a bag of garbage and heaved it onto the sidewalk. New Zealand mussel shells. Uneaten bits of portobello mushrooms. The fine grounds of decaf cappuccino.

One black plastic bag after another came out until Madison Avenue in front of 3 Guys was piled high with trash.

"Hurry up!" the young man shouted to the other Mexicans. "I want to go home, too."

9. When the Joneses Wear Jeans

JENNIFER STEINHAUER

Godiva sells luxury chocolates at 2,500 outlets, including this store on Madison Avenue in Manhattan. (Nicole Bengiveno/*The New York Times*)

It was 4:30 p.m., sweet hour of opportunity at the Beachwood Place Mall.

Shoppers were drifting into stores in the rush before dinner, and the sales help, as if on cue, began a retail ritual: trying to tell the buyers from the lookers, the platinum-card holders from those who could barely pay their monthly minimum balance.

It is not always easy. Ellyn Lebby, a salesclerk at Saks Fifth Avenue, said she had a customer who regularly bought $3,000 suits but "who looks like he should be standing outside shaking a cup."

At Oh How Cute, a children's boutique, the owner, Kira Alexander, checks out shoppers' fingernails. A good manicure usually signals money. "But then again," Alexander conceded, "I don't have nice nails and I can buy whatever I want."

Down the mall at the Godiva chocolate store, Mark Fiorilli, the manager, does not even bother trying to figure out who has money. Over the course of a few hours, his shoppers included a young woman with a giant diamond ring and a former airplane parts inspector living off her disability checks.

"You can't make assumptions," Fiorilli said.

Social class, once so easily assessed by the car in the driveway or the purse on the arm, has become harder to see in the things Americans buy. Rising incomes, flattening prices, and easily available credit have given so many Americans access to such a wide array of high-end goods that traditional markers of status have lost much of their meaning.

A family squarely in the middle class may own a flat-screen television, drive a BMW, and indulge a taste for expensive chocolate.

A wealthy family may only further blur the picture by shopping for wine at Costco and bath towels at Target, which for years has stocked its shelves with high-quality goods.

Everyone, meanwhile, appears to be blending into a classless crowd, shedding the showiest kinds of high-status clothes in favor of a jeans-and-sweatsuit informality. When

Vice President Dick Cheney, a wealthy man in his own right, attended a 2005 ceremony in Poland to commemorate the liberation of Nazi death camps, he wore a parka.

But status symbols have not disappeared. As luxury has gone down-market, the marketplace has simply gone one better, rolling out ever-pricier goods and pitching them to the ever-loftier rich. This is an America of $130,000 Hummers and $12,000 mother-baby diamond tennis bracelet sets, of $600 jeans, $800 haircuts, and slick new magazines advertising $400 bottles of wine.

Then there are the new badges of high-end consumption that may be less readily conspicuous but no less potent. Increasingly, the nation's richest are spending their money on personal services or exclusive experiences and isolating themselves from the masses in ways that go beyond building gated walls.

These Americans employ about nine thousand personal chefs, up from about four hundred just ten years ago, according to the American Personal Chef Association. They are taking ever-more exotic vacations, often in private planes. They visit plastic surgeons and dermatologists for costly and frequent cosmetic procedures. And they are sending their children to $400-an-hour math tutors, summer camps at French chateaus, and crash courses on managing money.

"Whether or not someone has a flat-screen TV is going to tell you less than if you look at the services they use, where they live, and the control they have over other people's labor, those who are serving them," said Dalton Conley, an author and a sociologist at New York University.

Goods and services have always been means to measure social station. Thorstein Veblen, the political economist who coined the phrase "conspicuous consumption" at the beginning of the last century, observed that it was the wealthy "leisure class," in its "manner of life and its standards of worth," that set the bar for everyone else.

"The observance of these standards," Veblen wrote, "in some degree of approximation, becomes incumbent upon all classes lower in the scale."

So it is today. In a 2005 poll by *The New York Times*, fully 81 percent of Americans said they had felt social pressure to buy high-priced goods.

But what Veblen could not have foreseen is where some of that pressure is coming from, says Juliet B. Schor, a professor of sociology at Boston College who has written widely on consumer culture. While the rich may have always set the standards, Schor said, the actual social competition used to be played out largely at the neighborhood level, among people in roughly the same class.

In the last thirty years or so, however, as people have become increasingly isolated from their neighbors, a barrage of magazines and television shows celebrating the toys and totems of the rich has fostered a whole new level of desire across class groups. A "horizontal desire," coveting a neighbor's goods, has been replaced by a "vertical desire," coveting the goods of the rich and the powerful seen on television, Schor said.

"The old system was keeping up with the Joneses," she said. "The new system is keeping up with the Gateses."

Of course, only other billionaires actually can. Most

Americans are staring across a widening income gap between themselves and the very rich, making such vertical desire all the more unrealistic. "There is a bigger gap between the average person and what they are aspiring to," Schor said.

But others who study consumer behavior say that the wanting and getting of material goods is not just a competitive exercise. In this view, Americans care less about emulating the top tier than about simply having a fair share of the bounty and a chance to carve out a place for themselves in society.

"People like having stuff, and stuff is good for people," said Thomas C. O'Guinn, a professor of advertising at the University of Illinois who has written textbooks on marketing and consumption. "One thing modernity brought with it was all kinds of identities, the ability for people to choose who you want to be, how you want to decorate yourself, what kind of lifestyle you want. And what you consume cannot be separated from that."

FALLING PRICES, RISING DEBT

Throughout the Beachwood Place Mall, located in an upscale suburb of Cleveland, Ohio, high-priced merchandise was moving: $80 cotton rompers at Oh How Cute, $40 scented candles at Bigelow Pharmacy. And everywhere, it seemed, was the sound of cellphones, one ringing out with a salsa tune, another with bars from Brahms.

Few consumer items better illustrate the democratization of luxury than the cellphone, once immortalized as the ultimate toy of exclusivity by Michael Douglas as he tromped around the 1987 movie *Wall Street* screaming into one roughly the size of a throw pillow.

Now, about one of every two Americans uses a cell-phone; in 2004, there were 176 million subscribers, almost eight times the number a decade earlier, according to the market research firm IDC. The number has soared because prices have correspondingly plummeted, to about an eighth of what they cost in 1994.

The pattern is a familiar one in consumer electronics. What begins as a high-end product—a laptop computer, a DVD player—gradually goes mass market as prices fall and production rises, largely because of the cheap labor costs in developing countries that are making more and more of the goods.

That sort of "global sourcing" has had a similar impact across the American marketplace. The prices of clothing, for example, have barely risen in the last decade, while department store prices in general fell 10 percent from 1994 to 2004, the federal government says.

Even where luxury-good prices have remained forbiddingly high, some manufacturers have come up with strategies to cast more widely for customers, looking to middle-class consumers, whose incomes have generally risen in recent years; the median family income in the United States grew 17.6 percent from 1983 to 2003, when adjusted for inflation.

One way makers of luxury cars have tapped into this market is by introducing cheaper versions of their cars, trying to lure younger, less-affluent buyers in the hope that they may upgrade to more prestigious models as their incomes grow.

Mercedes-Benz, BMW, and Audi already offer cars costing about $30,000 and now plan to introduce models that will sell for about $25,000. Entry-level luxury cars are the fastest-growing segment of that industry.

"The big new trend that is coming to the U.S. is 'subluxury' cars," said David Thomas, editor of Autoblog, an online automotive guide. "The real push now is to go a step lower, but the car makers won't say 'lower.'"

The luxury car industry is just one that has made its products more accessible to the middle class. The cruise industry, once associated with the upper crust, is another.

"The cruise business has totally evolved," said Oivind Mathisen, editor of the newsletter *Cruise Industry News*, "and become a business that caters to moderate incomes." The luxury end makes up only 10 percent of the cruise line market now, Mathisen said.

Yet today's cruise ships continue to trade on the vestiges of their upper-class mystique, even while offering new amenities like onboard ice skating and wall climbing. Though dinner with the captain may be a thing of the past, the ships still pamper guests with spas, boutiques, and sophisticated restaurants.

All that can be had for an average of $1,500 a week per person, a price that has gone almost unchanged in fifteen years, Mathisen said. The industry has kept prices down in part by buying bigger ships, the better to accommodate a broader clientele.

But affordable prices are only one reason the marketplace has blurred. Americans have loaded up on expensive toys largely by borrowing and charging. They now owe about $750 billion in revolving debt, according to the Federal Reserve, a sixfold increase from two decades ago.

That huge jump can be traced in part to the credit industry's explosive growth. Over the last twenty years, the industry became increasingly lenient about whom it was willing to extend credit to, more sophisticated about assessing credit risks, and increasingly generous in how much it would let people borrow, as long as those customers were willing to pay high fees and risk living in debt.

As a result, to take one example, millions of Americans who could not have dreamed of buying their own homes two decades ago are now doing so in record numbers because of a sharp drop in mortgage interest rates, a surge in the number of mortgages granted, and the creation of the sub-prime lending industry, which gives low-income people access to credit at high cost.

"Creditors love the term the 'democratization of credit,'" said Travis B. Plunkett, the legislative director of the Consumer Federation of America, a consumer lobbying group. "Overall, it has certainly had a positive effect. Many families that never had access to credit now do. The problem is that a flood of credit is now available to many financially vulnerable families and extended in a reckless and aggressive manner in many cases without thought to implications. The creditors say it has driven the economy forward and helped many families improve their financial lives, but they omit talking about the other half of the equation."

THE MARKETERS' RESPONSE

Marketers have had to adjust their strategies in this fluid world of consumerism. Where once they pitched advertisements primarily to a core group of customers—men earning $35,000 to $50,000 a year, say—now they are increasingly fine-tuning their efforts, trying to identify potential customers by interests and tastes as well as by income level.

"The market dynamics have changed," said Idris Mootee, a marketing expert based in Boston. "It used to be clearly defined by how much you can afford. Before, if you belonged to a certain group, you shopped at Wal-Mart and bought the cheapest coffee and bought the cheapest sneakers. Now, people may buy the cheapest brand of consumer goods but still want Starbucks coffee and an iPod."

Merchandisers, for example, might look at two golfers, one lower middle class, the other wealthy, and know that they read the same golf magazine, see the same advertisements, and possibly buy the same quality driver. The difference is that one will be splurging and then play on a public course while the other will not blink at the price and tee off at a private country club.

Similarly, a middle-income office manager may save her money to buy a single luxury item, like a Chanel jacket, the same one worn by a wealthy homemaker who has a dozen others like it in her $2.5 million house.

Marketers also know that today's shoppers have unpredictable priorities. Robert Gross, who was wandering the Beachwood mall with his son David, said he couldn't live without his annual cruise. Gross, who is sixty-five, also prizes his two diamond pinkie rings, his racks of cashmere sweaters, and his Mercedes CLK 430. "My license plate reads BENZ4BOB," he said. "Does that tell you what kind of person I am?"

But a taste for luxury goods did not stop Gross, an accountant, from scoffing as David paid thirty dollars for a box of Godiva chocolates for his wife. The elder Gross had been to a local chocolate maker. "I went to Malley's," he said, "and bought my chocolate half price."

Yet virtually no company that has built a reputation as a purveyor of luxury goods will want to lose its foothold in that territory, even as it lowers prices on some items and sells them to a wider audience. If one high-end product has slipped into the mass market, then a new one will have to take its place at the top.

Until the early 1990s, Godiva sold only in Neiman Marcus and a few other upscale stores. Today it is one of those companies whose customers drift in from all points along the economic spectrum. Its candy can now be found in 2,500 outlets, including Hallmark card stores and middle-market department stores like Dillard's.

"People want to participate in our brand because we are an affordable luxury," said Gene Dunkin, president of Godiva North America, a unit of the Campbell Soup Company. "For under a dollar to $350, with an incredible luxury package, we give the perception of a very expensive product."

But the company is also trying simultaneously to hold on to the true luxury market, which has increasingly been seduced away by small, expensive artisan chocolate makers, many from Europe, that are opening around the country. Two years ago, Godiva introduced its most expensive line ever, "G," handmade chocolates selling for $100 a pound. Today it is available only during holiday seasons and only at selected stores.

THE NEW STATUS SYMBOLS

While the rest of the United States may appear to be catching up with the Joneses, the richest Joneses have already moved on.

Some have slipped out of sight, buying bigger and more lavish homes in neighborhoods increasingly insulated from the rest of Americans. But the true measure of upper class today is in the personal services indulged in.

Dalton Conley refers to these less tangible badges of status as "positional goods." Consider a couple who hire a babysitter to pick up their children from school while they both work, he said. Their status would generally be lower than the couple who could pick up their children themselves, because the second couple would have enough earning power to allow one parent to stay at home while the other worked.

But the second couple would actually occupy the second rung in this after-school hierarchy. "In the highest group of all is the parent who has a nanny along," Conley said.

Status among people in the top tier, he said, "is the time spent being waited on, being taken care of in nail salons, and how many people who work for them." From 1997 to 2002, revenues from hair, nail, and skin care services jumped by 42 percent nationwide, Census Bureau data show. Revenues from what the bureau described as "other personal services" increased 74 percent.

Indeed, in some cases, services and experiences have replaced objects as the true symbols of high status. "Anyone can buy a one-off expensive car," said Paul Nunes, who with Brian Johnson wrote *Mass Affluence*, a book on marketing strategies. "But it is lifestyle that people are competing on more now. It is which sports camps do your kids go to and how often, which vacations do you take, even how often do you do things like go work for Habitat for Humanity, which is a charitable expense people can compete with."

In the country's largest cities, otherwise prosaic services have been transformed into status symbols simply because of the price tag. In New York, one salon introduced an $800 haircut, and a Japanese restaurant, Masa, opened in 2004 with a $350 prix fixe dinner (excluding tax, tips, and beverages). The experience is not just about a good meal, or even an exquisite one; it is about a transformative encounter in a Zen-like setting with a chef who decides what will be eaten and at what pace. And it is finally about exclusivity: there are only twenty-six seats. One of the most sought after status symbols in New York is a Masa reservation.

And that is how the marketplace works, Conley says. For every object of desire, another will soon come along to trump it, fueling aspirations even more.

"Class now is really like three-card monte," he said. "The moment the lower-status aspirant thinks he has located the nut under the shell, it has actually shifted, and he is too late."

10. The Five-Bedroom, Six-Figure Rootless Life

PETER T. KILBORN

Communities like Alpharetta, Georgia, have become havens for professionals and their families who relocate for work. (Nicole Bengiveno/*The New York Times*)

Kathy Link is forty-one with blond-streaked pigtails and, at five foot nine, straight as a spear. She is still in the red sun visor and tennis whites she wore leading her fitness class at the Forum Gym and winning at doubles afterward. Tucked by her seat is her color-coded itinerary.

Kaleigh, age eight, is red. With school over this afternoon

in late August 2004, she has already been dropped off at her soccer practice blocks from home. Kristina, age eleven, is dark green, and Kelsey, age thirteen, is yellow. Kristina must get to her soccer practice four miles to the north, and Kelsey to her practice fourteen miles to the south.

Kathy Link (blue for work, light green for family and volunteering) surveys the clotted intersection at the mouth of her 636-house Medlock Bridge subdivision in Alpharetta, Georgia. After moving here in 2001 and choking on traffic, she made a rule: "Wherever I'm going has to be within one mile of the house," she said. But she breaks the rule two or three times a day, driving ten and fifteen times the one-mile distance.

She squeezes the wheel of her white, eight-seat, leather-upholstered 2003 GMC Denali SUV. "Go, people," she pleads. Her knuckles go white. Twice she taps the horn. A timid driver in a gray van three cars ahead tiptoes into the Atlanta-bound avalanche along Highway 141. Link impatiently pulls abreast, saying, "I have to see who she is."

A rookie "relo," she decides, someone newly relocated to Alpharetta and to its traffic. She herself is a veteran relo, having moved three times in the past ten years to help keep her husband's career on track. She admits she is beginning to feel the strain of her vagabond life. "It's like I'm on a hamster wheel," she says.

Kathy and her husband, Jim, a forty-two-year-old financial services sales manager for the Wachovia Corporation of Charlotte, North Carolina, belong to a growing segment of the upper middle class, executive gypsies. The shock troops of companies that continually expand across the country and abroad, they move every few years, from St. Louis to Seattle to Singapore, one satellite suburb to another, hopscotching across islands far from the working class and the urban poor.

As a subgroup, relos are economically homogenous, with midcareer incomes starting at $100,000 a year. Most are white. Some find the salaries and perks compensating; the developments that cater to them come with big houses, schools with top SAT scores, parks for youth sports, and up-scale shopping strips.

Others complain of stress and anomie. They have traded a home in one place for a job that could be anyplace. Relo children do not know a hometown; their parents do not know where their funerals will be. There is little in the way of small-town ties or big-city amenities—grandparents and cousins, longtime neighbors, vibrant boulevards, home-grown shops—that let roots sink in deep.

"It's as if they're being molded by their companies," said Tina Davis, a top Alpharetta relo agent for the Coldwell Banker real estate firm. "Most of the people will tell you how long they'll be here. It's usually two to four years."

The Links bought their first home fifteen years ago in what was then the master planned community of Clear Lake City, Texas, now a part of Houston. In 1994, they moved to the old Baltimore suburb of Severna Park and three years later to Pittsford, New York, near Rochester. In another three years they bought a five-bedroom, four-bath home here, twenty-five miles north of Atlanta, where Jim Link started work at an office of the First Union Corporation, which became part of Wachovia.

THE POPULATION SPRAWLS

Still inching along, Kathy passes strip malls. She goes by the gym, chiropractors, nail shops, colonnaded stucco banks, hair salons, sixteen-pump gas stations, self-storage lots, Waffle Houses, a tanning place, and a salon that tattoos on lipstick and eyeliner so they will not fade in the pool.

She dodges the orange barrels of road-widening crews spreading asphalt in a futile effort to keep up with a north Fulton County population that has swelled to 273,000 from 170,000 in the 1990s, a decade when the city of Atlanta barely grew, to 416,000 from 394,000. Sidewalks start and stop. No one dares ride a bicycle or walk a dog. She crosses over Georgia 400, the clogged artery that pumps hundreds of thousands of commuters into Alpharetta's glass and brushed-metal office parks and, an hour's drive south, into downtown Atlanta.

She passes developments that from the air look like petri dishes of tadpoles, each tadpole head a cul-de-sac. In new subdivisions, signs in fancy script trumpet "price points," to show relos where to roost: Brookdale, $300s; Wildwood, $400s; Wolf Creek, $300s to $500s; Quail Hollow, $500s; Inverness, $600s to $800s; White Columns, $700s to $1.5 million; Greystone, $900s to $4 million.

The Hispanic landscaping crews are out with old Ford pickups tugging eight-foot flatbed trailers. They trim the edges of spongy Bermuda grass lawns and attack the grubs, fire ants, and weeds. Toys and even garden hoses are tucked out of sight lest the subdivision homeowners association issue warnings and fines. Garage doors, all motorized, must stay shut.

After dropping off Kelsey and Kristina, Kathy Link has to double back and pick up Kaleigh and take her to golf. She will wait for Kelsey to finish soccer before picking up Kristina and taking her to cheerleading practice. Another mother will have to retrieve Kristina so that Kathy can be home when Kaleigh's math tutor comes.

Jim (orange) cannot help. He is gone two to five days a week, to Boston, New York, Chicago, New Orleans, Dallas, and most often Charlotte. Monday and Tuesday, the itinerary says, "Jim in meetings, Charlotte." For Wednesday, it says, "Jim in meetings, Philadelphia."

A DIFFERENT SEGREGATION

Today's relos are the successors of itinerant white-collar pioneers of the 1960s, like the computer salesmen for whom IBM meant I've Been Moved. They are employees of multinational industry: pharmaceutical salespeople, electronic engineers, information technology managers, accountants, data analysts, plant managers, regional vice presidents, biotechnologists, bankers, manufacturers' representatives, and franchise chain managers.

They are part of a larger development that researchers are finding: an increasing economic segregation. A Brookings Institution analysis of census data last year reported that the percentage of people living in affluent or poor suburbs in fifty metropolitan areas increased from 1980 to 2000, and the percentage living in middle-income areas declined.

Just how many relos there are is hard to determine. The

tide rolls with corporate fortunes and the global economy, and relos are not singled out in census statistics. But in a survey from March 2002 to March 2003, the Census Bureau said that about three million people moved to another county, state, or country because employers had transferred or recruited them.

With the spread of global industry's new satellite office parks, the relos churn through towns like Alpharetta; Naperville, Illinois, west of Chicago; Plano, Texas, outside Dallas; Leawood, Kansas, near Kansas City; Sammamish, Washington, outside Seattle; and Cary, North Carolina, which is outside Raleigh and, its resident nomads maintain, stands for Containment Area for Relocated Yankees.

Converging on these towns, relos have segregated themselves, less by the old barriers of race, religion, and national origin than by age, family status, education, and, especially, income. Families with incomes of $100,000 head for subdivisions built entirely of $300,000 houses; those earning $200,000 trade up to subdivisions of $500,000 houses. Isolated, segmented, and stratified, these families are cut off from the single, the gay and the gray, and, except for those tending them, anyone from lower classes.

Unlike their upper-middle-class kindred—the executives, doctors, and lawyers who settle down in one place—relos forgo the old community props of their class: pedigree and family ties; seats on the vestry and the hospital board; and the rituals, like charity balls. Left with the class's emblematic cars, Lilly Pulitzer skirts and Ralph Lauren shirts, their golf, tennis, and soccer, and, most conspicuously, their houses, they have staked out their place and inflated the American dream.

"What is the American dream?" said Karen Handel, chairwoman of the Fulton County Commission in Alpharetta. "It's to have a house of your own, the biggest house you can afford, on the biggest lot you can afford, with a great school for your kids, a nice park to spend Saturday afternoon with your kids in, and deep in amenities that get into the trade-offs with traffic."

More so than the classes below and above them—the immobilized poor of old cities and rural backwaters, the factory-bound working class, and the old- and new-money rich—this is a fluid, unstable group. Those who lose jobs or decline promotions to let the children finish high school where they currently are sometimes relocate in place. They call the midnight movers to haul them to cheaper subdivisions, or seize the equity gains on their homes to move up.

The Link house stands on a cul-de-sac, up a slight rise with tall young oaks raining acorns over a small front yard and a curtain of cedar and pine bordering the back. It is three stories tall, with beige stucco walls and wide fieldstone panels flanking a varnished oak front door with leaded glass.

The house has a two-story family room hung with folk art, a room for guests that holds the girls' upright piano, a master suite upstairs with a bathroom with a wide, white vanity on each side of the door and a Jacuzzi enclosed in pinkish marble tiles. Three blocks away are the tennis courts, the pool, two soccer fields, and the two-story community clubhouse.

Alpharetta may be deep in Dixie, but its accent is not. Of the 30,000 people who live in the Links' census tract, 75 percent were born outside Georgia. Six percent are black, and

12 percent are Asian. Fewer than 3 percent are over sixty-five; fewer than 2 percent are poor or unemployed.

Two-thirds of the adults have had four or more years of college and earn more than $100,000 a year, twice the American family average. Their homes are worth an average of $400,000, twice the national average, and they have nearly twice as many rooms as the average house. "Everybody here is in the top ten percent of what they do," Steve Beecham, a home mortgage broker, said, "or they desire to be in the top ten percent."

In politics, Republican candidates are shoo-ins. Few Alpharetta lawns sprouted campaign signs during the last election season because the area's four contenders for the state legislature and a new candidate for Congress were all Republicans and ran unopposed.

JUST PASSING THROUGH

When the Links began house-hunting in early 2000, Jim Link said, "school was number one." After settling on the best school districts, he said, "we looked within price points." At their $300,000 limit, all they could afford in a good district near Atlanta was a three-bedroom, two-bath ranch-style house. "I wanted four bedrooms, two and a half baths, and a basement," Kathy Link said, "and I had to have a yard."

The house the Links eventually bought in Medlock Bridge, built in 1987, has 3,900 square feet and 1,100 more in a basement with a wall of windows facing the backyard. There is a recreation room with a bar, and a fifth bedroom.

"The basement is approximately the same size as my parents' entire house," Jim Link said. The Links paid $313,000 and took an 80 percent mortgage.

Pleased though they have been with the house, the Links never considered it permanent.

At the dishwasher one evening, Kathy said, "Jimmy has been saying, 'This travel is killing me.' I'm shocked we're still here. Every home we went to, I said, 'Could you sell this house?' I did not think we would be here four years. Early on, I told Jimmy, 'Wherever you choose to work, we will make a life.'"

"Jimmy's the one making the money. I want him to be happy and successful. Every area you move into, you buy into the lifestyle. Alpharetta is very big on tennis and soccer. We chose to participate in that."

Kathy's favorite place was Pittsford, an affluent apple-pie town outside Rochester with a congenial mix of transient families and long-settled ones. "Up there each town has its own little village and one main street where you can walk and ride your bike and get someplace safely," she said. Kelsey and Kristina started school and soccer there. Kathy became a certified personal trainer and began volunteering. She joined the Junior League.

CREATING THE ILLUSION OF HISTORY

The actual city of Alpharetta covers only twenty-three square miles in the northern half of Fulton County, but many subdivisions in adjoining unincorporated areas, like

Medlock Bridge, carry Alpharetta zip codes. The city has no real core, although it has a small downtown with a Main Street, City Hall, some restaurants, a Methodist and a Baptist church, two beauty parlors, a variety store, a new gift shop called Everything Posh, and a cemetery.

Just off Main Street, flanking an alley between two small parking lots, a pair of white wooden arches proclaim "Historic Downtown." But they lead only to the back walls of stores. Nearby is the Alpharetta Historical Society, housed in a hundred-year-old Queen Anne house. The house is a relo. A truck brought it up from Roswell in 1993.

"Illusionism is something that people have enjoyed for centuries," Diana Wheeler, the director of community development, said. "We're creating new applications. It's a matter of how it's carried out. It's a quality issue. You convert the illusion into something that has value to you. Maybe solid columns held up roofs, and hollow columns create the illusion they do. People will go to great lengths to impress others."

Tim Bryan builds illusions, designing million-dollar houses of at least 4,500 square feet. Bryan said clients "want it to look like a house that's evolved over a century, to appear to have been lived in for a hundred years or more, with the look of having been added on to." To achieve the look, a Bryan house may have a section of brick and next to it one of stone, then one of cedar shake.

With their price-pointed subdivisions, developers create pecking orders. "We're all busy looking down on each other," said Neal Martineau, a seventy-four-year-old retired advertising man who in the summer of 2004 was getting ready to move from just outside Alpharetta to West Virginia. " 'I'm better than you are and I'm going to show you.' It's a kind of bullying. It's architectural bullying."

"I'm faking it here," Martineau said. "I have property that does not have enough meadow to feed a horse, but I call it a horse farm."

"The car may be the most visible sign of status," he said. "My Mercedes is indicative of who I am. I am also a bit of a fraud. I probably shouldn't have a Mercedes, but I'm happy to wear a Mercedes. It's a way I have of making myself feel important, to have someone look at the best car on the road and know I'm in it."

One result of Alpharetta's subdivision-dotted terrain is the isolation of families from people unlike themselves. Zoning and planning are partly responsible, and so is the traffic. Except for the commute to work, the orbit of Medlock Bridge residents consists of the schools, the community pool, the tennis courts, the clubhouse, the shops along Medlock Bridge Road, and the St. Ives Country Club right across from the subdivision.

Atlanta seems so far away. "We haven't been to any cultural events or sporting events as a family because it's an all-night event," Jim Link said. People shop on the Internet. Rather than go to the car wash, they can call Tony Lancaster, who comes around in his van and brings the water, too. "Anything a shop can do, I can do mobile," Lancaster said.

Their seclusion helps keep the neighborhood safe, which is important to the Links. "We'll get a little rash of golf clubs stolen," Jim said. "Mailboxes have been hit or bent. We'll see where cars have gotten keyed. But that's about it.

"The good thing about it is that it is a very comfortable neighborhood to live in. These are very homogenous types of groups. You play tennis with them, you have them over to dinner. You go to the same parties.

"But we're never challenged to learn much about other economic groups," he said. "When you talk about tennis, guess what? Everybody you play against looks and acts and generally feels like you. It doesn't give you much of a perspective. At work, diversity is one of the biggest things we work on."

Alpharetta employers say that the $250,000 starting point for a detached, single-family house freezes out their secretaries and technicians, janitors and truck drivers, cashiers and data clerks. The prices exclude the city's own teachers and firemen. Of Alpharetta's 365 full-time city employees last fall, 112, or fewer than a third, lived in the city. Of seventy-four police officers, just the chief and two sergeants lived here.

House cleaners, like Linda Bates, live thirty or forty miles away. Bates works for Unlimited Cleaning Services, a company that supplies housekeepers with a checklist of the clients' requirements. A client may never speak to the cleaner or get the same one twice, and that is all right with Bates.

"If I have to be at a house at eight thirty I will leave my house at seven," she said. "We just clean the house and go, like the air-conditioning man. I never bother personal things. I never answer the telephone. I don't like being there when they get there."

ADJUSTING TO DIFFERENCES

Kathy Link came from Highland Park, an old planned community of what are now multimillion-dollar homes four miles north of downtown Dallas. Jim Link grew up in a Houston subdivision, Bellaire, in a house where his parents have lived for thirty-four years. They went to Texas A&M University in College Station, met at a student pub where Jim tended bar, and married three years later, in 1988. She found work as an editor for an aerospace company. Jim went into the insurance and mutual fund business, and from there he made the switch to banking.

Hardy, trim, and darker toned than his wife, in disposition still the affable bartender, Jim Link mans the beer cooler at holiday parties at the Medlock Bridge clubhouse. Kathy Link is more reserved. Her tennis doubles partner's high five is a slap. Hers is a tap. Often as she leaves the court one mother or another stops her and, taller than most, she settles an arm over the woman's shoulder as they walk. She pretends to have the time.

The Links agree on most things. In 2004 they voted for President Bush. They splurge on their children's sports and tutoring and piano lessons and deny them computers and televisions in their rooms and cellphones.

But her family was better off than his, and every now and then their views diverge on money. When he sees the occasional $140 charge for having her hair highlighted, she said, "he cringes."

"Kathy's goal for college for the kids," he said, "is like

her mother's was for her, that they not have to work." He worked, and it is fine with him if his children do.

She is happy in the $45,000 Denali that they financed. He is happy with the 2000 green Ford Taurus he bought used from CarMax for $10,000 in cash.

They are clear of the troubles with credit card debt that built up after Kelsey and Kristina were born. Jim earns something over $200,000, with bonuses based on the strength of the economy and his sales staff's success. Kathy earns around $4,000 from personal training and fitness instruction and plans to build on that as the children get older.

They have about $100,000 equity in the house and about $10,000 in college funds they started for the girls last year.

"We do all the basic stuff out of salary," Jim said. "Bonuses are free for everything else, like extra saving, big vacations, and major repairs on the house." Bonuses in 2004 bought the family their first ski trip, a week after Christmas in Steamboat Springs, Colorado.

For all their moving, the Links try to carry on an upper-middle-class tradition of volunteering and knitting community ties. Barely settled in Medlock Bridge, Jim ran for the board of the homeowners association and won. The board then made him president and, in effect, the mayor. He paid the $15,000 initiation fee for the family to join the St. Ives Country Club.

Kathy joined a neighborhood group to play bunko, a social dice game favored by Alpharetta women, many of whom think of it as an excuse to get together and have a few glasses of wine. She began editing the subdivision's newsletter and set up an e-mail chain that reaches 350 Medlock Bridge homes. She spends two hours on Tuesday mornings at a Bible-study meeting.

And she has bored into the schools. She became a vice president of the elementary school PTA and took on its newsletter. She is a room parent for Kaleigh's third-grade class and organizes science projects there. At her kitchen computer command post, she tracks the girls' reports and test scores on school Web pages. One of Kelsey's reports showed a 97 average, but then she got a 78 on a Spanish test. In a week, she had a tutor.

"The women are like the rulers," Kelsey said on a drive with her father during a weekend soccer tournament in Columbus, Georgia. "They have the big cars. The dads have the little cars and just go to work." She said her mother thought that her father was too relaxed on the road.

Jim said, "Kathy becomes impatient with me when I'm going seventy in a sixty-five zone."

"No, Daddy," Kelsey said. "It's when you're going sixty."

In the summer of 2004 Kathy's frenzied schedule began grinding her down. She gave up bunko. Then she dropped her PTA jobs and the community newsletter. A couple months later she was asked to lead a fund-raising drive for Kristina's cheerleading squad and said no. "I had never done that," she said.

But something else always seems to come up. She resumed editing the community newsletter because her successor gave it up. In November 2004 she learned of a school redistricting plan and shook her e-mail chain to mobilize opposition.

All her activity began creating tension at home. On the

sidelines of one of Kristina's soccer games, Jim said: "The single biggest thing to change is, Kathy has to be more judicious about how she volunteers. She would never give up Bible study. But she's now playing in three or four tennis leagues."

She agreed. "I volunteer way too much," she said.

"It doesn't mean you shouldn't be involved," he told her, "but it doesn't mean you have to be the leader."

UNEXPECTED CHALLENGES

The Links are the first to say they have not really found a way to make their Alpharetta life work. They found good schools, safe streets, neighbors they like, and a big house and a yard. But they did not count on the grueling traffic, on how far away everything seems, on how much is asked of volunteers to sustain the community, or on the stresses of a breadwinner's travels. They have no deep connections here, no old friends, no parents to sit for their children.

Kathy Link thinks about Highland Park, with her Presbyterian church and easy access to Dallas. She thinks about Rochester. "In Rochester," she said, "everything fell into place." In Alpharetta what weighs on her is just the daily grind.

"We haven't found a church," she said. "We went church shopping. I would find places my children liked and I didn't or that I liked and they didn't. We found one, but it's a half-hour drive away. We don't have that kind of time.

"It's all here, but it's an hour drive away. Here it's like, 'Get the heck out of my way.' It's like go, go, go. We're just going, going, going. I call it drowning. It's when you can't see the top of the water.

"In Rochester," she said, "you could go to festivals and street fairs, and museums and farms and pick your own apples and not have a death grip on your child. In Rochester I had two best friends," she added. "I don't have a girl best friend here in Alpharetta. There's no one person I can call up to confide in. I called up one girl, and I scared her."

EXPLORING A CHANGE

In the summer of 2003, Jim Link and Wachovia considered some organizational changes that might have led to a move for the family, but nothing came of them. In the summer of 2004 the discussions resumed, and that September he was promoted. Starting November 1, he became national sales manager for a broader range of the bank's money management services than he had been selling.

"It rounds me out," he said, folding laundry in the family room and watching a Georgia Tech football game on television. Whether to leave Alpharetta was left hanging, he said.

But they decided that the moving should stop for a while—nine years, at least, from the time Kelsey starts high school until Kaleigh finishes. With his BlackBerry, laptop, and access to the Hartsfield-Jackson Airport, Jim could do his new job from here. Wachovia leaves the choice up to him but tells him that moving to Charlotte should help his career.

"I told my boss, 'If you're willing to fund a full relocation package, I'm willing to do it,'" he said.

Back home from the family ski trip to Steamboat as 2004 ended, the Links seemed to be leaning toward one more move.

"I will remake myself to be a better mother and a better wife," Kathy said. "I've paid my dues."

Jim said: "We would try to be closer and more plugged in to the city. Kathy would continue volunteering, because that's how she gets involved. We would require that the kids be involved in something."

They were not telling friends, or the girls. Once word got around, they feared, teachers and coaches would start writing the girls off. Kelsey had figured it out. As they packed for Steamboat, Kathy said, Kelsey asked, "'Are we moving?' Jimmy couldn't lie. He said, 'It looks like it,'" and told her to keep mum.

They worry about Kristina. The shyest of the three girls, she was slow to take to Alpharetta. Then she bloomed. In her special-education reading class, she got 100s all fall and was moved to a regular class. She won her soccer team's Golden Boot award for scoring the most goals.

The Links called in Tina Davis, the real estate agent. Afternoons when the girls were in school, Kathy searched the Internet for homes and schools in Charlotte and found that it, too, was a sea of new subdivisions. The average commuting time is twenty-four minutes, the same as Atlanta.

Then she found Myers Park, a prosperous, close-in community of 8,700 where most of the houses are more than sixty years old and ten minutes from downtown. She found the Myers Park Presbyterian Church.

"It's like the one I went to in Highland Park," she said.

Jim Link got home from three days in Phoenix. He found a long e-mail message from Wachovia. "We got our paperwork," the relocation package, he said.

They told the girls after school. Kelsey took it easily, sad only that she would not be going to Northview High School with her friends. Kaleigh beamed, then frowned about losing friends and teachers.

Kristina was in the kitchen with Kathy when Jim came in.

"Your dad's got something to tell you," Kathy said.

"We're moving to Charlotte," he said.

Kristina paused. She would be leaving Rebecca, a friend of five years.

"I hate you," she said. "When?"

"In June," he said.

"What about soccer?"

She would keep playing here through May, they told her, and then get onto a team in Charlotte. She brightened a little.

That night Jim and Kathy went to dinner at Sia's, their favorite restaurant, just across Medlock Bridge Road.

"I'm happy," she said. "It's finally over. For four years, it's been when, when, when."

She told Jim: "I'm wired to settle in wherever we move and make a life for you and the family. But I still want a one-mile radius. I'm not going to do another Alpharetta."

By Kristina's twelfth birthday on April 16, 2005, pale green buds had broken out in the oaks in front of the Links' house. A landscaping crew was setting pink and white petunias into the new pine straw mulch around the shrubs. Inside, floors had been sanded and the master bath retiled in beige limestone. "Finished basement," the red headline on Tina Davis's sign out front said.

Jim left early that day to take Kelsey to a soccer game thirty miles away. Kathy and Kristina watched Kaleigh's Green Gators near home.

"Go, Kaleigh!" Kathy shouted. "Get in the middle, Kaleigh. Go!"

On the sidelines, a father turned to her.

"Kathy, what's this I hear you're leaving?"

"We are," she said.

"Work stuff?"

"Wachovia," she said. "Charlotte."

"We're going to miss you," he said.

"It's kind of bittersweet," she said. "We want to be there nine years, but you never know."

In May 2005, the Links sold their house in Alpharetta for $420,000 and bought a Cape Cod in Charlotte for $627,500. It is half the size of the one in Alpharetta, but it is in leafy old Myers Park. The Myers Park Country Club, the Presbyterian church, and top-rated public schools are less than a mile away.

On a visit to their new home, the girls got library cards. They tried out for a soccer club and all three made the cut. They would move in July.

11. Old Nantucket Warily Meets the New

GERALDINE FABRIKANT

Nina Chandler Murray remembers the gentility and discipline that marked status for Nantucket's "old money" generation. (Ruth Fremson/The New York Times)

In spring, along with the daffodils, crowds on the ferry, and workers raking the beaches, comes the ritual of real estate gossip. What properties changed hands over the winter? And who could possibly be paying those out-of-sight prices?

That fifteen-acre waterfront parcel for sale for $15 million? It was snatched up after only one day on the market. Turns out the purchaser was Steven Rales, the billionaire entrepreneur who owns at least sixty-one acres next door and bought the parcel to protect his privacy and waterfront views, said Dalton Frazier, a local real estate agent.

Have any other palatial estates expanded? Not so long ago H. Wayne Huizenga, the billionaire founder of Blockbuster and owner of the Miami Dolphins, wanted more elbow room and bought a neighboring house for $2.5 million. Richard Mellon Scaife, the publisher and heir to a banking fortune, bought an extra house, too; he needed it for the staff.

The real estate frenzy, even in the dead of winter, is only the most visible reminder that over the past decade or so Nantucket, a fifty-square-mile, fishhook-shaped island off the Cape Cod coast, has come to be dominated by a new class: the hyper-rich. They emerged in the 1980s and 1990s, when tectonic shifts in the economy created mountains of wealth. They resemble the arrivistes of the Gilded Age, which began in the 1880s when industrial capitalists amassed staggering fortunes, except that there are so many of them and they seem to be relatively anonymous.

Like their precursors, they tend to be brash, confident, and unapologetic. They feel they have earned their money, and they are not shy about spending it. They construct huge mansions, outdo one another in buying high-end status symbols like mega-yachts (one hundred years ago it was private railroad cars), and not infrequently turn to philanthropy. Their wealth is washing over the upper reaches of society as it did a century ago, bringing cultural and political clout as they take up positions on museum boards and organize presidential campaign fund-raising dinners.

And they seem unconcerned about being accepted by the old money. If the blue bloods want to mix with them, fine. But if not, the hyper-rich are content to stick with their kind. If they cannot join an exclusive country club, they form their own. They are very good at creating a self-enclosed world where the criterion for admission is not the Social Register, but money.

Once a low-key summer resort, Nantucket is rapidly turning into their private preserve, joining the ranks of other enclaves like Palm Beach, Aspen, the Hamptons, and Sun Valley. Now that the hyper-rich have achieved a critical mass, property values have zoomed so high that the less-well-off are being forced to leave and the island is becoming nature's ultimate gated community.

"It's a castle with a moat around it," said Michael J. Kittredge, a fifty-three-year-old entrepreneur who realized a fortune when he sold his Yankee Candle Company in 1998 for about $500 million. He was relaxing in the living room of his 10,000-square-foot house, which has a basement movie theater and a two-thousand-bottle wine cellar. A separate residence a quarter-mile away houses staff members and a gym.

"Successful people want to be with other successful people," Kittredge said. "Birds of a feather," he added. "On Nantucket you don't feel bad because you want a nice bottle of wine. If you order a three-hundred-dollar bottle in a restaurant, the guy at the next table is ordering a four-hundred-dollar bottle."

Dressed in blue jeans and a pink button-down shirt, he

looked across the breadth of his swimming pool at a spectac-
ular water view. The island, he said, is rapidly dividing into
two types of people: "the haves and the have-mores."

NEW-FASHIONED VALUES

Nantucket, with its vistas overlooking cranberry bogs and
more than eighty miles of beaches, has always had its share
of rich people. In the first half of the nineteenth century,
owners of whaling ships amassed fortunes from oil and built
the still well-preserved Federalist and Greek Revival mansions on upper Main Street.

During the last century, Vanderbilts, Mellons, duPonts,
and other wealthy families built residences here. Over time,
as inherited wealth smoothed the rough edges, their descen-
dants morphed into American high society and evolved a
signature style of living based on understatement and old-
fashioned patrician values.

Some of the scions of these older families are still here.
They spend their time sailing, playing tennis, and sometimes
recalling the halcyon days of crossing the moors behind
packs of beagles to hunt down rabbits. The mix of the old
aristocratic families and the hyper-rich often plays out as a
none-too-subtle tug-of-war between class and money.

Nina Chandler Murray, an eighty-five-year-old relative
of the Poor family of Standard & Poor's, the investment
credit rating firm, is convinced that the world of the elite was
more genteel in the old days.

"Coming from a New England background, you had a

honed discipline of what was expected," Murray, a psychologist, said over iced tea and chocolate chip cookies on the porch of her hillside home above the harbor. "Showing off money was a sin. It was not that status was not important, but marriage was very closely controlled and predetermined, and everyone knew where everyone else fit."

A family name alone was enough to place someone in the pecking order. Wealthy people dressed down. Women eschewed heavy jewelry. The uniform for a man was a plain shirt, faded "Nantucket red" Bermuda shorts, and Topsiders. Now, Murray suggested, the rule is: If you've got it, flaunt it.

"What has happened in America is that achievement is so important that everyone wants everyone else to know what they have done," she continued. "And in case you don't know, they want to tell you with a lethal combination of houses, cars, and diamonds."

Murray was appalled at a recent dinner party when a woman leaned over to her and said, "My husband paid $250,000 to join the golf club, and he doesn't even play golf."

WORK HARD, SPEND HARD

Michael Kittredge, who began his candle-making business at age sixteen in his mother's kitchen and says he was raised in a "lower-class to lower-middle-class" home, holds attitudes typical of many of the newcomers. When prodded he will say that he worked hard for his money and that others can do the same. He is unapologetic about spending it lavishly and says that he has paid his dues in the form of taxes, which he estimates at $500 million so far. He also says that the chasm between the old-timers and the newcomers is inevitable.

"Money makes a lifestyle," he said. "It creates a division between the old money and the new. It is a little bit of class jealousy. We go to a cocktail party and a guy is telling my wife about his airplane. So finally the question comes up: 'How do you get over to the island?' and she says, 'We come by plane.' And he says, 'What kind of plane?' and she says, 'A G-IV.' And so the wind comes out of the guy's sails.

"The old money guy has a twin-prop airplane and that is pretty incredible," Kittredge continued. "For his time, that is pretty great. Now he is talking to a guy who is half his age who has a transcontinental jet. That is the end of the conversation.

"Or you meet someone and they start telling you about their boat. He has a forty-five-foot boat and he is very happy with it. Then he'll say, 'Do you have a boat?' And you say, 'Yes.' 'Well, what kind of boat do you have?' And you say, 'A Fead Ship.' And he says, 'How big is it?' That's how people rank them. So I have to say, 'It's two hundred feet.' It's the end of the conversation. Is there envy? Yes, could be. Was he a wealthy guy in his day? Absolutely, but relative to today—no. The two worlds can mix as long as they don't talk too much."

The accoutrements of wealth play a different role for the old-money clans than they do for the new wealthy, says Nelson W. Aldrich Jr., author of *Old Money*.

"For many self-made men," Aldrich said, "homes, boats, and even membership in expensive clubs are trophy signs of wealth. But for the older money, a boat may well be part of a tableau that has to do with family, with his grandparents and his children. It is part of his identity. If he walked away from the conversation, it was because he thought he was talking about his boat as part of his life. Instead he found he was talking about money, and he doesn't like being reminded that he lives in a competitive world."

Over time, some say, the new money will not prove much different. "Ultimately, the new money becomes as insular as the old money because it gains the power to exclude," said Michael Thomas, a novelist who, like his father, was a partner at Lehman Brothers and whose mother came from an old New England family. "Once you have the power to exclude, you have what people have been seeking in old money."

The single greatest change brought by the hyper-rich is in the cost of housing. The average Nantucket house price last year jumped 26 percent, to $1.672 million, said H. Flint Ranney, a veteran real estate broker.

In the fall of 2004 one waterfront residence, with its own elevator, wine cellar, theaters, and separate guesthouse, sold for $16 million, the year's record.

"Shame has somehow gone out the window," Thomas said. "There is no incentive to exercise control."

A handful of the new affluent indulge their fantasies with gusto. Michael S. Egan, the founder of Alamo Rent-a-Car, built his own baseball field, complete with a batting cage and stands. Roger Penske, the automotive tycoon and former race car driver, tussled for months with the Historic

District Commission until he finally won permission to build a faux lighthouse that joins the two wings of his multimillion-dollar home. The investment banker Robert Greenhill likes to fly his Cessna jet to the Nantucket airport or his Cessna seaplane to his waterfront dock.

The rise in real estate values has, of course, benefited many of the old-timers. With some of their fortunes erod-ing, they find they are sitting on an extremely valuable asset, a realization that adds a touch of ambivalence to their protests against changes that are all too obvious.

One such change is at the airport. On high summer weekends, more than 250 Challengers, Gulfstreams, and Ci-tations a day might land there, vying for parking spaces. Some jets drop off passengers for a round of golf and whisk them away after.

In easternmost Siasconset, the gray-shingled fishermen's cottages that occupied the corners of plots of sea grass and wildflowers are giving way to mansions in private cul-de-sacs. Here and there hedges have sprouted up, tall as Wind-surfers, to partition the property parcels. They separate the community, contributing to the ineffable sense that some-thing familiar and precious about the ethos of the island is disappearing.

"At least one new family has built a hedge to avoid peo-ple seeing them as they pass by," said Wade Green, seventy-two, who has summered here for years. "Those open paths had an old-fashioned elegance to them. It is part of an old and fading spirit of community. Blocking them off is an un-friendly and antipublic thing to do."

Not all the changes here are striking. Downtown, with its cobblestone streets and absence of traffic lights, could still pass as a quaint New England fishing village. But some harbingers horrify the old-timers: upscale restaurants, boutique windows displaying expensive designer jewelry, and the arrival of the first-ever chain store, a Ralph Lauren shop.

On the sidewalks, class speaks through clothes. "The old money wears Lilly Pulitzer, J. McLaughlin, and CK Bradley," said one saleswoman, who wanted her name withheld to avoid offending customers. "They wear gold hoops, and if they buy new jewelry it is pearls or they upgrade their diamond rings. The new money wears Juicy Couture, Calypso, and big necklaces. They even go to different restaurants. The old people go to 21 Federal and the new people go to the Pearl. They don't want to mix. They want to show off for each other."

But the lines cross. A handful of the hyper-rich gravitate toward Lilly Pulitzer to give themselves a blue-blood look. And some pedigreed teenagers lust for Juicy Couture.

Daisy Soros, wife of the harbor designer Paul Soros and sister-in-law of the financier George Soros, has been coming to Nantucket since the 1960s, an era when few women, new money or old, dressed up. She thinks that the newcomers are beginning to influence the culture.

"Everybody is building monster houses now, and they are all dressing up," Soros said. "Now even I wear Manolos," she added with a laugh.

Some say that too much is being made of all these distinctions. "The only people who are truly class conscious," said

Roger Horchow, who realized his fortune when he sold his catalog business to Neiman Marcus in 1988 for $117 million, "are the second tootsie wives of men with big bankrolls."

WHY WAIT? BUILD A NEW ONE

When there is a division between the old and the new, it is apt to express itself on the most time-honored of battlefields: the putting green, the tennis court, or the marine berth.

The existing clubs are still the preserves of the old wealth, but new clubs are springing up to welcome newcomers, as well as some longtime residents who grew impatient with waiting lists. For years the Sankaty Head Golf Club had a waiting list that seemed to extend for decades. So in 1995, Edmund A. Hajim, an investment banker in Manhattan, and others created the Nantucket Golf Club, assiduously designed to look as if it had been around forever. It became such a hit that its list is now full, too, even at a cost of $325,000 (80 percent reimbursable upon departure), as opposed to the $30,000 it costs to join Sankaty Head.

In the same way, the old Nantucket Yacht Club has spawned a rival, the Great Harbor Yacht Club. About three hundred families have already bought memberships, which now cost $300,000.

Some Nantucketers applaud the new clubs.

"Why shouldn't they start a club if they can't get into the old ones," said Letitia Lundeen, who was raised in the social whirl of New York and Washington and now runs an antiques store here.

The resentment of new money riles Liz Petkevich, whose husband, J. Misha Petkevich, an investment banker and former Olympic figure skater, helped found the new yacht club. Her husband worked hard for what he achieved, she said. "Does that mean we are better than anyone else? No. But we should not be penalized because we cannot get into the old yacht club."

In the old days, the clubs were homogenous and dominated by white Anglo-Saxon Protestant families.

"When I first came here it was the tail end of the 'grande dame' era," said David L. Hostetler, a sculptor, who arrived in 1971. "The place was dominated by WASP women in Bermuda shorts. There were hardly any Jews."

Today the island's elite is diversified enough to support a synagogue where membership has reached 250 families and where the yarmulke worn during services is Nantucket red and decorated with miniature whales.

One place where the old and the new do mix is charity events. As in cultural and philanthropic institutions from San Francisco to New York City, the old money has made room at the table for the new money to replenish the coffers. There are more and more fund-raising events, and they are no longer the low-key affairs they once were. In 2004 the annual cocktail party and auction for the Nantucket Historical Association instituted valet parking and a classical quartet in black tie.

Some appreciate the infusion of money and energy that the newcomers have brought. "The old money doesn't like to spend money because they worry about whether they can make it again," Lundeen said. "Even when they can spend it, they often think it's vulgar and unnecessary. The newcomers have brought the island up to par with their demands."

EVERYTHING NEW IS OLD

Old-time Nantucketers are given to trading what one of them called "barbarian stories." Did you hear that Rick Sherlund, a Goldman Sachs partner, annoyed some of his neighbors when he hired Jackson Browne to entertain at his anniversary party? Or that Jon Winkelried, another Goldman Sachs partner, had the nerve to close off a small road that people had been using for as long as anyone can remember? Or that Louis V. Gerstner, the former IBM chief executive, hired a Boston litigator to help him push through a plan for a large new house on his $11 million waterfront plot?

Aggressive behavior, Nina Murray said, is natural to the species. "And after all, why should they give it up?" she said. "Look where it has gotten them. That is exactly how they made their money."

One Nantucketer was L. Dennis Kozlowski, the former chief executive of Tyco International, who in 2005 was convicted on charges of criminal larceny. His lavish New York apartment, with its $6,000 shower curtain, became a symbol of the over-the-top corporate lifestyle.

To some, the multimillion-dollar party that Kozlowski gave on Sardinia to celebrate his wife's birthday—replete with a vodka-spewing ice sculpture fashioned after Michelangelo's *David*—was a modern echo of the lavish celebrations of the Gilded Age.

Subtler distinctions between old and new money lie in the attitude toward work. The financier David Rubinstein bought a fifteen-acre waterfront property, tore down the existing house, as many wealthy buyers have done, and put up an 8,000-square-foot home. The stunning view lets him watch the sun rise and set, and yet he has boasted to friends that he spends only twelve days a year here; a rock on his front lawn reads: "I'd rather be working."

Robert E. Torray, who is a co-manager of a mutual fund family and has been flying here on his company's Gulfstream since the 1980s, is either on the golf course or working the phone in his cranberry-red library. He likes it here because there are Wall Street moguls everywhere and wherever he goes he can talk business.

That is hardly the attitude of some veteran summer residents, who find comfort in the thought that they can occasionally be fogged in without worrying about the office. For them, being rich means a license to break schedules and to play. "If you are working," said Nicki Gamble, whose husband, Richard, is an heir to the Procter & Gamble fortune, "it is very nerve-racking. The way to be here is not to be working."

CAUGHT BY A BOOM

The high cost of housing is squeezing middle-class people off the island.

The former principal of Nantucket High School, Paul Richards, and his wife, Martina, a nurse, moved last year to

Needham, Massachusetts, after renting here for five years. "The expense of that together with having two little children made a home beyond reach," Richards said. "It was frustrating to be driven away from two jobs that we very much enjoyed, but a starter home for our family would have cost over $600,000."

Linda Finney Williams, administrator of the Nantucket Zoning Board of Appeals, who has a nineteen-year-old son in college and an older daughter in law school, said, "I'm hanging on by my fingernails. The cost of living has risen so much that it's very hard on us."

The demand for labor is so great that every weekday roughly four hundred workers fly in from the mainland for construction, gardening, plumbing, and other services. The commute may be a nuisance, but the money makes it worthwhile. It also explains why building is so expensive; the additional costs are passed along to customers.

John Sheehan, a sixty-five-year-old construction worker who rises every day at 4:30 a.m. to catch a plane from Hyannis, does not complain. "I have always been in the lower-middle-class area," he said. "But the times are good for me now. I'm making more money than I ever did and I'm living more comfortably."

To try to stem the outflow of workers the Nantucket Housing Office, a private nonprofit group, has proposed a one-time "McMansion" tax of eight dollars per square foot on any construction space exceeding 3,000 square feet. The bill has several more hurdles, but if it is approved, the proceeds would be used to build housing for families making

$120,825 a year or less. Some real estate agents worry that the hyper-rich will resent the tax, but so far wealthy home-builders seem to regard it as a pittance compared with the other costs they incur.

Despite the money to be made, some shop owners and other locals miss the way the island used to be.

Though she applauds their self-confidence, Letitia Lundeen, the antiques dealer, says she is sometimes appalled by what she considers the cavalier ignorance of some women who are suddenly rich. "They don't want to learn," she said. "I had a monogrammed tray and when I proposed it to a customer, she said, 'Why would I want other people's monograms?' These women have never inherited anything."

Robin Bergland, a young florist who moved here from Manhattan, has stopped providing flowers for weddings. "The final straw was a wedding where a Wall Street executive tried to bill me for the wedding gown and medical expenses," she said. "He charged that the roses I used to decorate their party tent ruined the hem of the bride's dress and caused her aunt to trip and break her leg.

"I got threatening phone calls daily. I was terrified until I gave the case to my lawyer and they went away. There's no question it was unlikely to have happened five years ago."

The old summer people "used to try and fit in," said Arlene Briard, a taxi driver who has lived here thirty-five years. "They didn't want to differentiate themselves by class or by a look that said how much money I have. When I sold *TV Guide* to people, I'd walk into a house, sit down, and have a lemonade with people or play tennis with them at the yacht club. Now they get in my taxi and find a way to tell me that they belong to the Nantucket Golf Club.

"Class has a certain grace," Briard said. "Just because you can go to Chanel and buy a dress does not mean you have class. A person who just pays their bills on time can have class."

12. Richest Are Leaving Even the Rich Far Behind

DAVID CAY JOHNSTON

When F. Scott Fitzgerald pronounced that the very rich "are different from you and me," Ernest Hemingway's famously dismissive response was: "Yes, they have more money." Today he might well add: much, much, much more money.

The people at the top of America's money pyramid have so prospered in recent years that they have pulled far ahead of the rest of the population, an analysis of tax records and other government data by *The New York Times* shows. They have even left behind people making hundreds of thousands of dollars a year.

Call them the hyper-rich.

They are not just a few Croesus-like rarities. Draw a line under the top 0.1 percent of income earners—the top one-thousandth. Above that line are about 145,000 taxpayers, each with at least $1.6 million in income and often much more.

The average income for the top 0.1 percent was $3 million in 2002, the latest year for which averages are available. That number is two and a half times the $1.2 million, adjusted for inflation, that group reported in 1980. No other income group rose nearly as fast.

The share of the nation's income earned by those in this uppermost category has more than doubled since 1980, to 7.4 percent in 2002. The share of income earned by the rest of the top 10 percent rose far less, and the share earned by the bottom 90 percent fell.

Next, examine the net worth of American households. The group with homes, investments, and other assets worth more than $10 million comprised 338,400 households in 2001, the last year for which data are available. The number has grown more than 400 percent since 1980, after adjusting for inflation, while the total number of households has grown only 27 percent.

The Bush administration tax cuts stand to widen the gap between the hyper-rich and the rest of America. The merely rich, making hundreds of thousands of dollars a year, will shoulder a disproportionate share of the tax burden.

President Bush said during the third election debate in October 2004 that most of the tax cuts went to low- and middle-income Americans. In fact, most—53 percent—will go to people with incomes in the top 10 percent over the first fifteen years of the cuts, which began in 2001 and would have to be reauthorized in 2010. And more than 15 percent will go just to the top 0.1 percent, those 145,000 taxpayers.

The *Times* set out to create a financial portrait of the very richest Americans, how their incomes have changed over the decades, and how the tax cuts will affect them. It is no secret that the gap between the rich and the poor has grown, but the extent to which the richest are leaving everyone else behind is not widely known.

Not Since the Twenties Roared

The very wealthiest Americans—the 145,000 or so taxpayers whose incomes start at $1.6 million and put them in the top 0.1 percent—have pulled away from everyone else in recent decades, an analysis by *The New York Times* shows.

GROWTH IN INCOME

The share of the nation's income earned by the taxpayers in the top 0.1 percent has more than doubled since the 1970s, and in the year 2000 exceeded 10 percent, a level last seen in the 1920s.

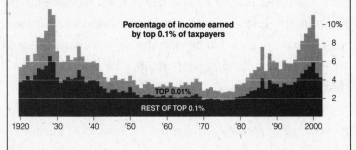

Percentage of income earned by top 0.1% of taxpayers

TOP 0.01%

REST OF TOP 0.1%

GROWTH IN WEALTH

Even after adjusting for inflation, there are five times as many households as there were two decades ago with a net worth of more than $10 million. Not all have high incomes.

Number of households	ALL HOUSEHOLDS	$1–5 MILLION	$5–10 MILLION	$10 MILLION+
		Households with inflation-adjusted net worth of:		
in 1983	84 million	2.2 million	180,500	66,500
in 2001	106 million	4.8 million	729,400	338,400
Percent increase	**+27%**	**+123%**	**+304%**	**+409%**

The U.S. Treasury Department uses a computer model to examine the effects of tax cuts on various income groups but does not look in detail fine enough to differentiate among those within the top 1 percent. To determine those differences, the *Times* relied on a computer model based on the Treasury's. Experts at organizations representing a range of views, including the Heritage Foundation, the Cato Institute, and Citizens for Tax Justice, reviewed the projections and said they were reasonable, and the Treasury Department said through a spokesman that the model was reliable.

The analysis also found the following:

- Under the Bush tax cuts, the four hundred taxpayers with the highest incomes—a minimum of $87 million in 2000, the last year for which the government will release such data—now pay income, Medicare, and Social Security taxes amounting to virtually the same percentage of their incomes as people making $50,000 to $75,000.

- Those earning more than $10 million a year now pay a lesser share of their income in these taxes than those making $100,000 to $200,000.

- The alternative minimum tax, created thirty-six years ago to make sure the very richest paid taxes, takes back a growing share of the tax cuts over time from the majority of families earning $75,000 to $1 million—thousands and even tens of thousands of dollars annually. Far fewer of the very wealthiest will be affected by this tax.

The analysis examined only income reported on tax returns. The Treasury Department says that the very wealthiest find ways, legal and illegal, to shelter a lot of income from taxes. So the gap between the very richest and everyone else is almost certainly much larger.

The hyper-rich have emerged in the last three decades as the biggest winners in a remarkable transformation of the American economy characterized by, among other things, the creation of a more global marketplace, new technology, and investment spurred partly by tax cuts. The stock market soared; so did pay in the highest ranks of business.

One way to understand the growing gap is to compare earnings increases over time by the vast majority of taxpayers—say, everyone in the lower 90 percent—with those at the top, say, in the uppermost 0.01 percent (now about 14,000 households, each with $5.5 million or more in income last year).

From 1950 to 1970, for example, for every additional dollar earned by the bottom 90 percent, those in the top 0.01 percent earned an additional $162, according to the *Times* analysis. From 1990 to 2002, for every extra dollar earned by those in the bottom 90 percent, each taxpayer at the top brought in an extra $18,000.

President Ronald Reagan signed tax bills that benefited the wealthiest Americans and also gave tax breaks to the working poor. President Bill Clinton raised income taxes for the wealthiest, cut taxes on investment gains, and expanded breaks for the working poor. President George W. Bush eliminated income taxes for families making under $40,000, but his tax cuts have also benefited the wealthiest Americans far more than his predecessors' did.

The Bush administration says that the tax cuts have actually made the income tax system more progressive, shifting the burden slightly more to those with higher incomes. Still, an Internal Revenue Service study found that the only taxpayers whose share of taxes declined in 2001 and 2002 were those in the top 0.1 percent.

But a Treasury spokesman, Taylor Griffin, said the income tax system is more progressive if the measurement is the share borne by the top 40 percent of Americans rather than the top 0.1 percent.

The *Times* analysis also shows that over the next decade, the tax cuts Bush wants to extend indefinitely would shift the burden further from the richest Americans. With incomes of more than $1 million or so, they would get the biggest share of the breaks, in total amounts and in the drop in their share of federal taxes paid.

One reason the merely rich will fare much less well than the very richest is the alternative minimum tax. This tax, the successor to one enacted in 1969 to make sure the wealthiest Americans could not use legal loopholes to live tax-free, has never been adjusted for inflation. As a result, it stings Americans whose incomes have crept above $75,000.

The *Times* analysis shows that by 2010 the tax will affect more than four-fifths of the people making $100,000 to $500,000 and will take away from them nearly one-half to more than two-thirds of the recent tax cuts. For example, the group making $200,000 to $500,000 a year will lose 70 percent of their tax cut to the alternative minimum tax in 2010, an average of $9,177 for those affected.

But because of the way it is devised, the tax affects far fewer of the very richest: about a third of the taxpayers reporting more than $1 million in income. One big reason is that dividends and investment gains, which go mostly to the richest, are not subject to the tax. Another reason that the wealthiest will fare much better is that the tax cuts over the past decade have sharply lowered rates on income from investments.

While most economists recognize that the richest are pulling away, they disagree on what this means. Those who contend that the extraordinary accumulation of wealth is a good thing say that while the rich are indeed getting richer, so are most people who work hard and save. They say that the tax cuts encourage the investment and innovation that will make everyone better off.

"In this income data I see a snapshot of a very innovative society," said Tim Kane, an economist at the Heritage Foundation. "Lower taxes and lower marginal tax rates are leading to more growth. There's an explosion of wealth. We are so wealthy in a world that is profoundly poor."

But some of the wealthiest Americans, including Warren E. Buffett, George Soros, and Ted Turner, have warned that such a concentration of wealth can turn a meritocracy into an aristocracy and ultimately stifle economic growth by putting too much of the nation's capital in the hands of inheritors rather than strivers and innovators. Speaking of the increasing concentration of incomes, Alan Greenspan, the Federal Reserve chairman, warned in congressional testimony in 2004: "For the democratic society, that is not a very desirable thing to allow it to happen."

Others say most Americans have no problem with this trend. The central question is mobility, said Bruce R. Bartlett, an advocate of lower taxes who served in the Reagan and George H. W. Bush administrations. "As long as people think they have a chance of getting to the top, they just don't care how rich the rich are."

But in fact, economic mobility—moving from one income group to another over a lifetime—has actually stopped rising in the United States, researchers say. Some recent studies suggest it has even declined over the last generation.

About the data used in the chart on pages 190–91: The calculations come from four sources. The data on income growth come from government tax return records analyzed by Emmanuel Saez, economics professor at the University of California, Berkeley, and Thomas Piketty, economics professor at the École des Hautes Études en Sciences Sociales in Paris. The data on wealth come from the Federal Reserve's Consumer Finance Survey, analyzed by Edward Wolff, a professor of economics at New York University. The estimates of taxes come from a computer model of the Tax Policy Center, a joint project of the Urban Institute and the Brookings Institution, and include income, corporate estate taxes, and proposals in President George W. Bush's 2006 budget to extend the cuts indefinitely. The data on the four hundred highest-income taxpayers come from an Internal Revenue Service report, with 2004 tax rules applied to 2000 data. All data are the most recent available.

Links to the data sets used in the analysis are available at http://www.nytimes.com/class.

The Wealthiest Benefit More From the Recent Tax Cuts

Under the recent tax cuts, the richest taxpayers get the largest break, in dollars and in the drop in their share of all federal taxes paid. That is because those taxpayers benefit most from lower taxes on dividends and investment gains, and because the alternative minimum tax, which was originally intended to apply only to the very richest people, now takes back a large portion of the tax cuts of people who are not the richest. "Taxpayers" refers to both single and joint filers.

| Percentile | BOTTOM 80 PERCENT | | | | TOP 20 PERCENT | | | | | | Top 400 taxpayers (Also included in top 0.1%) |
	Bottom	20–40	40–60	60–80	80–90	90–95	95–99	99–99.5	99.5–99.9	Top 0.1	
Income in **2005**	$0–13,478	$13,478–25,847	$25,847–44,451	$44,451–79,562	$79,562–117,001	$117,001–162,351	$162,351–383,407	$383,407–581,019	$581,019–1,589,608	$1,589,608 or more	$87 million or more*
Taxpayers	28 million	30 million	29 million	29 million	14 million	7.2 million	5.8 million	723,000	578,000	145,000	400
Share of taxpayers	19.5%	20.6%	19.9%	19.9%	10.0%	5.0%	4.0%	0.5%	0.4%	0.1%	0.0003%
Share of nation's reported income in **2001**	2.5%	6.4%	11.7%	20.1%	15.8%	11.2%	15.0%	3.8%	5.9%	8.0%	1.1%*
Share of federal taxes that would have been paid in **2001** *without cuts*	0.4%	2.6%	8.6%	17.9%	16.0%	12.3%	17.5%	4.8%	7.9%	12.0%	Data not available
Share of federal taxes to be paid in **2015** *with cuts*	0.5%	2.7%	7.9%	17.9%	16.6%	13.0%	18.5%	4.6%	7.4%	10.8%	Data not available

The groups that see their share of federal taxes decline by 2015 are those in the top 1 percent and those in the middle.

The New York Times

		Less than $30,000	$30,000–50,000	$50,000–75,000	$75,000–100,000	$100,000–200,000	$200,000–500,000	$500,000–$1 million	$1 million–10 million	More than $10 million	Top 400 taxpayers
Share of tax cut over fifteen years	0.3%	5.3%	9.5%	16.4%	15.5%	9.8%	12.5%	5.4%	10.1%	15.2%	Data not available
Average yearly tax savings	$23	$342	$618	$1,063	$2,202	$2,101	$4,051	$14,107	$32,767	$195,762	$8.3 million
Percentage of income paid in income, Social Security, and Medicare taxes in 2004		6.7%	14.5%	17.4%	18.9%	20.6%	21.6%	21.6%	22.3%	20.1%	17.5%

Taxpayers making $100,000 to $200,000 now pay a greater share of their income in income and payroll taxes than those making more than $10 million.

THE STEALTH TAX

A growing number of people making more than $75,000 will have much of their cuts taken back by the alternative minimum tax

	Less than $30,000	$30,000–50,000	$50,000–75,000	$75,000–100,000	$100,000–200,000	$200,000–500,000	$500,000–$1 million	More than $1 million	All taxpayers
Percent paying A.M.T. in 2004	Under 1%	Under 1%	Under 1%	1%	6%	50%	39%	27%	2%
In 2010	Under 1%	3%	16%	52%	80%	94%	63%	36%	22%
How much of group's cuts taken	Under 1%	Under 1%	3%	23%	47%	70%	23%	9%	29%
Extra tax paid by those affected	$1,429	$773	$942	$1,560	$2,542	$9,177	$15,727	$64,025	$3,579

* For 2000.

The New York Times

13. In Fiction, a Long History of Fixation on the Social Gap

CHARLES McGRATH

It Happened One Night *was one of a number of movies during the Depression to examine romance across the class divide.* (Everett Collection)

On television and in the movies now, and even in the pages of novels, people tend to dwell in a classless, homogenized American Never-Never Land. This place is an upgrade, but not a drastic one, from the old neighborhood where Beaver,

Ozzie and Harriet, and Donna Reed used to live; it's those yuppified city blocks where the friends on *Friends* and the *Seinfeld* gang had their apartments, or in the now more fashionable version, it's part of the same exurb as One Tree Hill and Wisteria Lane—those airbrushed suburbs where all the cool young people hang out and where the pecking order of sex and looks has replaced the old hierarchy of jobs and money.

This is progress of a sort, but it's also repression, since it means that pop culture has succeeded to a considerable extent in burying something that used to be right out in the open. In the old days, when we were more consumed by social class, we were also more honest about it.

There is an un-American secret at the heart of American culture: for a long time, it was preoccupied by class. That preoccupation has diminished somewhat—or been sublimated—in recent years as we have subscribed to an all-purpose, mass-market version of the American dream, but it hasn't entirely disappeared. The subject is a little like a ne'er-do-well relative; it's sometimes a shameful reminder, sometimes openly acknowledged, but always there, even, or especially, when it's never mentioned.

This was particularly true in the years before World War II, when you couldn't go to the movies or get very far in a novel without being reminded that ours was a society where some were much better off than others, and where the class divide—especially the gap separating middle from upper—was an inescapable fact of life. The yearning to bridge this gap is most persistently and most romantically evoked in

Fitzgerald, of course, in characters like the former Jay Gatz of Nowhere, North Dakota, staring across Long Island Sound at that distant green light, and all those moony young men standing in the stag line at the country club, hoping to be noticed by the rich girls.

But there is also a darker version, the one that turns up in Dreiser's *An American Tragedy*, written in 1925, for example, where class envy—a wish to live like his rich tycoon uncle—causes Clyde Griffiths to drown his hopelessly proletarian sweetheart, and where the impossibility of transcending his lot leads him inevitably to the electric chair. (In the upstate New York town of Lycurgus, where the story takes place, Dreiser reminds us that "the line of demarcation and stratification between the rich and the poor was as sharp as though cut by a knife or divided by a high wall.")

Some novels trade on class anxiety to evoke not the dream of betterment but the great American nightmare: the dread of waking up one day and finding yourself at the bottom. This fear gets an earnest and moralizing expression in early books like P. H. Skinner's 1853 novel, *The Little Ragged Ten Thousand, or, Scenes of Actual Life Among the Lowly in New York*, which is pretty much summed up by its title. By the turn of the century, though, in works like Stephen Crane's *Maggie: A Girl of the Streets* and Frank Norris's *McTeague*, about a San Francisco dentist who, unmasked as a fraud, sinks to a life of crime and degradation, the treatment had turned grim and unflinching.

These books were frankly meant to shock their middle-class readers—to scare the daylights out of them—even as they played on their sympathies. They suggested that the worst thing that could possibly happen to an American was to topple from his perch on the class ladder, as happens to poor Hurstwood in Dreiser's *Sister Carrie*. In his besotted pursuit of Carrie (who meanwhile trades on her beauty and charm to move up from her Chicago boardinghouse to the bright lights of Broadway), he loses everything and crashes all the way from restaurant-owning prosperity to scabbing for work as a trolley car driver.

The poor are noticeably absent, however, in the great artistic flowering of the American novel at the turn of the nineteenth century, in the work of writers like Henry James, William Dean Howells, and Edith Wharton, who are almost exclusively concerned with the rich or the aspiring middle classes: their marriages, their houses, their money, and their stuff. Not accidentally, these novels coincided with America's Gilded Age, the era of overnight fortunes and conspicuous spending that followed in the wake of the Civil War.

To a certain extent James, Wharton et al. were merely writing about the world around them, though in James there is sometimes a hint of aesthetic snobbery, a sense that refined writing required a refined subject matter. (In *The Ambassadors*, for example, he explains that the Newsomes made their fortune in manufacturing, but can't quite bring himself to be so vulgar as to tell us exactly what they made.) In Wharton and Howells, on the other hand, there is frequently an edge of satire, and sometimes a hint of seismic rumble.

Wharton's most vivid characters are not the aristos, the sons and daughters of the great New York families, who are all a little bloodless and sexually underpowered, but people like Lily Bart, whose lifestyle outstrips her pocketbook and who winds up in economic free fall. And then there are the climbers and the nouveaus, people like Undine Spragg in *The Custom of the Country*, who arrives in New York from provincial Apex City, Kansas, determined to rise up in society the old-fashioned way—by marrying, which she does not just once but three times, if you count the one that was supposed to be a secret. One of the messages of the novel is that in America new money very quickly, in a generation or less, takes on the patina of old; another is that the class structure is necessarily propped up by deceit and double standards.

But to a generation of writers after Wharton that structure—the lives and mores of the rich, the wellborn, and the climbers—proved endlessly diverting. Young men and women on the make, and older ones trying anxiously to cling to their perch, throng an entire bookcase full of American fiction.

John O'Hara, for example, made a whole career of chronicling the upper and upper middle classes from before the First World War until after the Second, and no one ever observed more astutely the little clues that indicated precisely where one stood on the class ladder: the clubs and fraternity pins, the shoes, the shirt collars. J. P. Marquand pored over much the same territory and, like O'Hara, became both a popular and a critical success. Every now and then a racy book about lowlife—*Tobacco Road*, for example—would catch the public fancy, but for a surprisingly long time middle-brow fiction in America was about upper-middle-class life.

What was the appeal? Vouyerism, in part. (It didn't hurt O'Hara's sales one bit that he saw it as part of his mission to inform us that upper-class people had very busy sex lives.) Fiction back then had a kind of documentary function; it was one of the places Americans went to learn about how other Americans lived. In time novels ceased to be so reportorial, and after the Second World War, moreover, as the middle class in America swelled in numbers and importance, the world of the upper crust lost some of its glamour and importance.

The old kind of class novel—about striving and trying to move up by learning the upper-class code—is still being written. *Prep*, a first novel by Curtis Sittenfeld, about an ambitious scholarship girl who finds herself in over her head, smoldering with class resentment, at a school that closely resembles Groton, became a surprise bestseller in 2005. But more often the upper class is portrayed these days as a little beleaguered and merely trying to hang on, like the members of the New England family in Nancy Clark's 2003 novel *The Hills at Home*, all failures in one way or another, who have retreated back to the ancestral manor, or like Louis Auchincloss's Wasp lawyers and businessmen, who have a sense of themselves as the last of a breed.

Elsewhere in the fictional landscape, a number of young writers—short-story writers especially—are still working in the afterglow of our once very hot literary romance with the world of Wal-Marts and trailer parks, so vividly evoked in the writing of Raymond Carver, Bobbie Ann Mason, and Frederick Barthelme, among others. But to a considerable extent novels these days take place in a kind of all-purpose middle-class America, in neighborhoods that could be almost anyplace, and where the burdens are more psychic than economic, with people too busy tending to their faltering relationships to pay much attention to keeping up with the neighbors.

It's a place where everyone fits in, more or less, but where, if you look hard enough, nobody feels really at home. Our last great middle-class hero, someone who really enjoyed his vacations and his country club, was John Updike's Rabbit Angstrom, and he died a premature death. Nowadays when a writer like Richard Russo, Russell Banks, or Richard Price comes along, with an old-fashioned, almost Dickensian vision of life among the poor and working classes, it's a little startling; they seem like explorers who have returned from some distant land.

Novel reading is a middle-class pastime, which is another reason that novels have so often focused on the middle and upper classes. Mass entertainment is another matter, and when Hollywood took up the class theme, which it did in the 1930s, it made a crucial adjustment. During the Depression, the studios, which were mostly run by immigrant Jews, turned out a string of formulaic fantasies about life among the Gentile upper crust.

These movies were essentially twin variations on a single theme: either a rich young man falls for a working girl, as happens in, say, *Easy Living*, to take one of many examples, or an heiress takes up with a young man who has to work for a living (in a number of cases he's a newspaperman, which was Hollywood's idea of a truly disreputable profession back then).

Joan Crawford made a specialty of the working girl role, in movies like *Sadie McKee* and *Dancing Lady*, and also did the heiress in *Love on the Run* and *I Live My Life*. But the great example of this genre is *It Happened One Night*, with Claudette Colbert and Clark Gable, who famously dispensed with wearing an undershirt.

It Happened One Night implicitly answered the question of what an upper-class woman got in return for trading down: great sex. In other versions of the story the upper-class person is merely thawed and humanized by the poorer one, but in every case the exchange is seen as fair and equitable, with the lower-class character giving as much as he or she gets in return. Unlike the novels of class, with their anxieties and sense of unbridgeable gaps, these are stories of harmony and inclusion, and they added what proved to be an enduring twist on the American view of class: the notion that wealth and privilege are somewhat crippling conditions—if they don't make you an out-and-out twit, they leave you stiff, self-conscious, and emotionally vacant until you are blessed with a little lower-class warmth and heart.

The formula persisted right up through movies like *Love Story* and *Pretty Woman*, though it seems to be in disuse now that films, like novels, are increasingly set in an upscale, well-scrubbed America where Wasps are an endangered, pitiable species. Like the in-laws in *Meet the Fockers* and *My Big Fat Greek Wedding*, they are still hopelessly uptight but not that wealthy anymore.

Television used to be fascinated with blue-collar life, in shows like *The Honeymooners, All in the Family, Sanford and Son,* and *Roseanne,* but lately it too has turned its attention elsewhere. The only people who work on televison now are cops, doctors, and lawyers, and they're so busy they seldom get to go home. The one vestige of the old curiosity about how other people live is in so-called reality television, when Paris Hilton and Nicole Richie drop in on rubes in *The Simple Life,* or when upper- and middle-class families trade moms on *Wife Swap* and experience a week of culture shock.

But most reality television trades in a fantasy of sorts, based on the old game-show formula: the idea that you can be plucked out of ordinary life and anointed the new supermodel, the new diva, the new survivor, the new assistant to Donald Trump. You get an instant infusion of wealth and are simultaneously vested with something far more valuable: celebrity, which has become a kind of super-class in America, and one that renders all the old categories irrelevant.

Celebrities, in fact, have inherited much of the glamour and sexiness that used to attach itself to the aristocracy. If Gatsby were to come back today, he would come back as Donald Trump and would want a date not with Daisy but with Britney. And if Edith Wharton were still writing, how could she not include a heavily blinged hip-hop mogul?

But if the margins have shifted, and if fame, for example, now counts for more than breeding, what persists is the great American theme of longing, of wanting something more, or other than what you were born with—the wish not to rise in class so much as merely to become classy. If you believe the novels of Dickens or Thackeray, say, the people who feel most at home in Britain are those who know their place, and that has seldom been the case in this country, where the boundaries of class seem just elusive and permeable enough to sustain both the fear of falling and the dream of escape.

14. Angela Whitiker's Climb

ISABEL WILKERSON

Angela Whitiker with some of her children. Clockwise from lower left are Willie, Johnathan, Christopher, Ishtar, and her husband's son, Zachary. (Ozier Muhammad/*The New York Times*)

Angela Whitiker arrived early and rain-soaked at a suburban school building with a carton of sugar water in her purse and a squall in her stomach. It was the small hours of the morning, when the parking lot was empty and the streetlights were still on. There she was alone in the darkness for the biggest test of her life.

If she passed, she could shed the last layer of her former

self—the teenage girl who grew up too fast, dropped out in the tenth grade, and landed aimless and on public assistance with five children by nearly as many men.

She would finally be the registered nurse she had been striving toward for years. She could get a car that wouldn't break down in the middle of Chicago's Dan Ryan Expressway. She could get an ATM card and balance her checkbook and start paying down her bills and save up for that two-story colonial on Greenwood that was already hers in her dreams.

She would never again have to live in that gang-run nightmare of a place, the Robert Taylor housing projects—where she packed a .38 for protection—or in Section 8 housing or in any government-subsidized anything. Her children could be proud of her and go on to make something of themselves, too, once she proved it could be done.

But if she didn't pass. . . .

She couldn't think about that. And so, as she would often tell the story later, she got up before dawn and made herself some oatmeal and a hard-boiled egg and toast and got to the testing site for the state licensing boards for registered nurses two hours before the test began.

She had never been good at tests. All through nursing school, she agonized the night before an exam, overstudying the charts and graphs, termites dropping from the ceiling onto her physiology books, mice crawling at her feet, and her children tugging her leg to find out what was for dinner.

She had only recently become the first woman in her family with a college degree and, if everything went well this day, would be the first nurse anybody in her family knew personally.

So, she left long before she needed to that morning to avoid traffic, a missed turn, not enough gas. Once there, she sat parked in the rain trying to compose herself. She pulled out her Bible to read the 91st Psalm, the one about the Lord being her refuge. She broke out the sugar water to get glucose to the brain.

In the hallway, she avoided looking anyone in the eye. She spoke to no one. She didn't want to pick up on anyone's anxiety. She had enough of her own. She took a last drag on a Newport.

The testing room began to fill. The examiner checked her identification and assigned her computer No. 12. She drew in another deep breath as she walked to her place. She was about to sit down to take a $256 pass-or-fail entrance exam into the American middle class.

For most of her thirty-eight years, Angela Whitiker has been on the outside looking in at the seeming perfection of the professional classes, the people who did the college-career-wedding-house-in-the-suburbs-2.5-kids routine. Her life has been so very different from that. She was a child of the working class who, through ill-considered choices and circumstance, slipped into the welfare class and had to fight her way out.

While the rest of the country has fitfully cut back welfare and continues to debate class disparities and the barriers to mobility, Whitiker has quietly traversed several classes in a single lifetime. She has gone from welfare statistic in the early 1990s to credit card–carrying member of the middle class, a woman for whom there are now few statistics, so rare has her experience been. This is the story of her twelve-year slog to the middle class and of how hard it is to stay there.

The third of five children, she was born to a mother who was a cook and to a laborer father whom, though the parents had married, she didn't meet until she was ten. She said it was a heartbreaking visit in which, smelling of whiskey, he promised to buy her a bicycle and didn't. She hasn't seen him since.

Within a few years, she was using men as a substitute for her father and her adolescent longing for him. By fifteen, she was pregnant with her first child. By twenty-three, she was the mother of five children, had been married and separated, and been a casualty of the crack epidemic of the 1980s. She had lost and would later win back custody of her children, and had worked a variety of odd jobs, from sausage vendor to picking butterbeans.

At twenty-six, she gained short-lived celebrity when she and her oldest son, Nicholas, then a ten-year-old fourth grader with a man's obligations, were the subjects of a profile by this reporter in *The New York Times*, part of a 1993 series on at-risk urban young people called "Children of the Shadows."

She, Nicholas, and her four other children were living in a second-floor walk-up in Englewood, a crime-burdened neighborhood abandoned first by the white middle class and then by the black middle class that succeeded it.

For her, each day meant trying to piece together enough to take care of herself and her kids—one day petitioning the fathers for child support, the next counting what was left of her food stamps; one minute rushing to an administrator's office to get bus vouchers for school, the next bargaining with the electric company to get her lights turned back on.

To keep her family out of the projects and on what might be described as the upper rung of poverty, she had taken up with a man who worked handling baggage at O'Hare International Airport. He paid the rent and was the father of her fifth child, Johnathan. His paycheck gave her breathing room to get into a pre-nursing program at Kennedy-King Community College on the South Side.

But men never seemed to hang around that long, and it fell to Nicholas to be father to the younger children that the men in their lives seemed unwilling to be.

He was the one who washed his and his siblings' school uniforms in the bathtub at night because they each had only one set. He was the one who pulled his brother Willie out of the line of fire by the hood of his jacket when gunshots rang out in the school yard. And he was the one who took the blame and the beatings if something wasn't done to his mother's boyfriend's liking.

Readers responded with great outpourings of generosity after the article was published, but it was clear from the reporter's continuing contacts with the family over the years that it was not enough to materially change the basic facts of their lives. It was still a household run by a single mother with only a high school equivalency degree, no career skills, no assets, and no immediate prospects for independence.

In addition, the fraying relationship between Whitiker and her boyfriend fell apart and, without him to pay the rent, she fell further behind. She wound up in the only place that a woman with five children, no job, and no money could get in Chicago in 1994, a cellblock of an apartment in the Robert Taylor Homes, an urban no-man's-land where you could move about only when the gangs that ran the place let you. The elevators, sticky with urine, didn't work, and gunshots were background music.

From the start, Whitiker felt that it was beneath her. She looked down on the women who had grown accustomed to bullet holes over their dinette tables, who watched *All My Children* and ate Doritos all day and didn't seem to want anything better. She carried the gun to protect herself and had to use it once when, having climbed nine flights of stairs, she found some strangers playing cards at her kitchen table. She fired shots into the ceiling to get them out.

It was the lowest rung of the poverty class in America, lower in a way than the worst nights in a crack house in her early twenties, because now she was fully conscious of exactly where she was. She vowed from the very first night to get out. But she knew she couldn't make it out on public assistance. So she figured she'd get whatever job she could. She would have to put off her nursing studies.

She worked at a fast-food restaurant, rising to assistant manager but never making much more than minimum wage. She worked nights as a security guard in the projects, a job that was dangerous and equally dead end but paid a bit more.

Every day held its own kind of peril or indignity, much of it coming from her 1976 Chevrolet, which she relied on to get to and from work but was well past its natural life span. It had a cracked windshield and a hole rusted through the floor. It wasn't big enough for all of her children, but they piled in just the same with no thought of seat belts, because there weren't enough anyway.

When she was coming home in the rain on the express-way one night, the defroster conked out and the windshield fogged up. "I had to stick my head out the window to drive," she said. "God drove that car that night."

One time the car caught fire because of a hole in the gasoline line. Flames shot out of the hood and into the air. Whitiker jumped out and told her sister, Michelle, riding in the passenger seat, to do the same.

"Get out of the car!" she screamed. "It's gonna blow!"

A fire truck came to put out the fire. The firefighters argued over which one should try to start the engine. None of them wanted to. So she had to try herself. Somehow, it started and got her home, just another day on her long climb out of the hole.

The drug economy played out every day on the cracked concrete lawns of Robert Taylor, and her preteen older sons, Nicholas and Willie, could not help breathing it in. The only workingmen they saw were the drug dealers who were up early to meet their sales quotas, wore the latest gym shoes, and got the girls. Their cars were new and didn't catch fire.

The family lived at Robert Taylor for nine months. "It was hell," she would say later. "I wouldn't want a dog to stay up in there."

She left there a new woman. She knew she had to get back into nursing school if she was ever going to get anywhere.

LEARNING A NEW WAY

Then she met a man by the name of Vincent Allen. He wasn't like the other men she had known. He had a college degree. His father had been a military man, his mother a homemaker, solidly middle class. He had a nice apartment with floor-to-ceiling windows overlooking Lake Michigan. Whitiker was struck by his manners and how he spoke like the teachers and social workers she had known growing up— enunciating his words, slipping in a few she didn't know. He was a police detective.

They met on the job when they were working as private security guards. He took an immediate liking to her, saw that they both wanted the same thing—in his words, a "picket fence kind of a life." He encouraged her to follow her dreams. Soon she and the kids were moving in with him. He took his job as the man of the house seriously and actually liked the father role. Suddenly, there was a man asking about homework and where Nicholas and Willie had been. He noticed if they had slipped on some gang colors or had their caps pushed to the left or the right as gang members did.

He took it upon himself to correct the behavior of the younger children and pick them up from school.

That had been Nicholas's job for all of his short life, and, as his mother recalled, he did not take displacement well. First, she said, he figured he would scare his rival away. He stole his clothes, talked back, came in late.

It would only be a matter of time before this man would go the way of all the other men, Nicholas thought. But Vincent Allen did not leave. And the sweet little boy who had been the father of his family went out and found a new family in the streets. The drug dealers were more than willing to take him and put him to work. Before long, Whitiker discovered that her twelve-year-old Nicholas was a lookout for the dealers.

She and Allen could see the road Nicholas was on, but, streetwise though they were, could do little to stop it. The more vigilant Allen was, the more resentful and alienated Nicholas became, and the worse things got. It was as if he had grown so accustomed to the chaos of his mother's previous lives that he did not know how to function when a family worked as it should. He had made himself into a wind gauge and had no purpose when the air was still.

Whitiker sent Nicholas to live with his father, a laborer who had married, had other children, and lived on the other side of town. She hoped that being far from his homies would put Nicholas on a straighter course.

Allen started encouraging her to go back to nursing school. They figured that, with him providing a place for her to live, and with Pell grants and the other financial aid for low-income students, she could make a go of it.

She enrolled at Kennedy-King College again, but it was different this time; or, rather, she was different. She was no longer the fun-loving girl looking for something to do. She had seen the bottom of the well and never wanted to go back there again.

She had also seen a new way of managing one's life. The professional people she met in college and now Allen had different ways of thinking about spending and saving money and carrying oneself. They tended to plan and save for things. She had never had enough money or reason to save. They paid attention to things like late fees and interest rates; she mostly ignored them because she couldn't pay the bills anyway. They set long-term goals for themselves; she just tried to get through the day. It all rubbed off on her, and it changed her.

On top of that, she had a renewed sense of time pressing against her. How long would Allen put up with her and the kids while she went to school? What if he got tired of it and left? What if he insisted she quit school and get a job to pay her share of the expenses? She didn't like the idea of owing him and couldn't bear the thought of slipping backward again. So, when it came to her studies, she would have to be more focused and efficient than she had been about anything in her life.

"I HAD TO MAKE IT"

There were certain points in certain years—say from 1996 to 2002—when Angela Whitiker didn't yet know that Tupac Shakur had been killed or that President Bill Clinton had been impeached.

"If it wasn't about nursing or biology or what was on my test Friday, I wasn't interested," she said. "I blocked everything and everybody out. I used to be so particular about cleaning the house. I got to the point where I'd see a shoe, and I'd just kick it over."

She felt she had to work extra hard because she felt so outranked in the classroom. She endured the stares of the middle-class teacher's pets who looked down on her for the circuitous route that got her there. "They were snobs whose moms were nurses, and they knew everything," she said. "I had to show them that I was somebody, that because I had five kids, that I made bad decisions, that I didn't have a father—and so what?—I was determined to show them I can do this. I had to make it. I couldn't fail."

Whenever test day came, she recalled, she would work herself into such a state of anxiety that sometimes she had to excuse herself to throw up. The professor had to go get her out of the bathroom.

"Are you okay?" the professor would ask. "You're going to kill yourself."

Everybody knew when a test didn't go well. They could see it in her face, the simultaneous pouting and rolling of the eyes, and hear it in her voice, the way she snapped at the lowest registers over the littlest thing.

"Mama didn't pass her test today," the first child to notice would say to the others. "Don't say nothing."

Because she wasn't from a professional family, she brought a kind of naïveté to school with her. One day in a clinical class, she recalled, the teacher went around the room asking students how their patients were doing. When the teacher got to her, Whitiker thought about the colostomy bag attached to her patient and started crying.

"Oh my God," the teacher said. "Did your patient die?"

"No," she said, still sobbing. "But she had this hole in her stomach."

"Well, go on in there and wash your face," the teacher told her.

Soon she was working with cadavers as if they were just another piece of office equipment, but she didn't know anyone who could give her the ins and outs of the field or tell her what to expect. "I didn't have anybody I could go to who had a degree other than Vince," she said. He went over her papers and marked them up—too much for her liking, sometimes—and read her papers aloud so she could hear what was wrong with them.

When she made the dean's list, he celebrated. When she failed a test, he consoled her as best he could.

"Oh baby, you're going to make it," he'd say.

"Oh shut up, you don't understand," she'd shoot back.

In May 2001, she finally finished nursing school at

Kennedy-King, one of the City Colleges of Chicago. For her class picture, she wore her hair in a flip like Gidget and a nurse's cap that looked like white dove wings. It was a long way from the teenager in jheri curls and too-tight jeans.

Soon she would be driving in the rain to take the nursing boards on computer No. 12. "It was a step to another life," she would say years later. "It was a do-or-die type of thing. I thought I was going to kill myself waiting for the results."

THE TEST RESULTS

One morning in late 2001, when Whitiker was alone and the apartment was uncharacteristically quiet, the mail arrived and, in it, an envelope from the state boards. In that moment, she came closer than at any other time of her life to upper-middle-class young people awaiting word from the Ivy League school of their dreams. The chatter among her fellow nursing students was that a thin envelope meant you passed; a thick one, presumably filled with the things you got wrong, meant you failed. She got a thin envelope.

"My heart just dropped to the floor," she said. She took the envelope into the apartment and threw it on the bed, afraid to open it, afraid that, given the disappointments of her life, somehow the grapevine had been wrong and the thin one meant failure.

She called her mother to get the courage to open it. Soon she was out in the middle of the hallway. "I passed my boards!" she screamed to neighbors fumbling for their house keys.

The family took her out to celebrate. They had dinner at Hooters and bought her a cake. Soon after, she and Allen agreed it was time they married.

"My daughter was getting to an age where I was trying to tell her to do right," Whitiker said of Ishtar, now seventeen. "I can't tell her to do right if I'm doing wrong."

They married at Faith Temple Coptic Church on June 7, 2003. She wore an ivory shift and a long white veil and carried a bouquet of white carnations. He wore a black tux. It was the groom's first marriage, the bride's second.

All the kids were there except Willie, who, still on the path he learned at Robert Taylor, was in jail. The remaining kids were dressed to their mother's specifications, except Nicholas, who, having by now declared that he wanted to be a rapper, showed up in pants hanging off his body and a baseball cap turned backward.

For the family wedding picture, his mother told him to stand in the back so nobody could see what he had on. She was already becoming class conscious, aware of appearances and decorum. And so, on this triumphant day in the family's history, all that is visible of Nicholas is his head.

HIGH-STRESS WORK

Whitiker finished nursing school as vice president of her class and with academic awards in biology and pharmacology, but despite her hard work and potential, the reality of her life was that she could not afford to go any further than a two-year associate's degree. That limits her job prospects even in a high-demand field like nursing. She doesn't have the contacts to get a job at the teaching hospitals in Chicago where she would get better training and higher pay.

She landed a job at a small inner-city hospital on the South Side, known not for its groundbreaking procedures or training opportunities but as the hospital where the eight student nurses killed by Richard Speck in 1966 had worked. It's an unnerving history that is always in the back of her mind, but she needs the job and the pay is more than she could ever have imagined back when she was on food stamps.

She has worked high-stress assignments in telemetry— monitoring cardiac patients—and in the intensive care unit. With all the night hours she puts in, she made $83,000 last year, more than 90 percent of all American workers. It is hard work, messy, often thankless. She has found herself in a pecking order that surprises and frustrates her. The doctors seem to expect her to work magic on their orders, she said, and the certified nursing assistants resent her place of privilege.

A few years back she might have sympathized with the nursing assistants. They do what no one else wants to do, attending to the unpleasant bodily needs of the very ill. There was a time when that would have been a move up for her. But their envy and resentment only made her feel more distant. And now, she was showing the same disdain for them that the middle class might have felt for her in her other life.

"I'm like, don't be mad at me because I'm a nurse," she said. "If you want my job, you need to suffer and cry like I did."

She tried to find her bearings in this new class she was in.

She resented the old friends who drank muscatel at the taverns late into the night and hit her up for money. And yet her past had a way of catching up with her in unexpected ways. She was out running errands once when a man recognized her from her days on the street.

"I know you," he said. "You're the one who stole money from me."

She feigned ignorance and walked away, even though, she would later say, she remembered taking his money and his television set, too, back when she was on drugs.

She tried hanging out with the nurses from work. But some were bourgeois and uppity, had a sense of comfort and confidence she did not possess. At one party she went to, some of them started smoking marijuana. It was a fun little escape for them, but it took her back to a place she could not afford to revisit.

"I reached for my purse," she said. "When I got my first paycheck, that was high enough for me."

Her life was complicated as it was. For one thing she was now the mother of six (seven, if you counted Zach, her husband's thirteen-year-old son, who recently moved in with them). Her youngest, Christopher, had been born shortly after the uncertain time at Robert Taylor and had been with her only off and on because of a custody fight between her and Christopher's father.

Both the fight over Christopher and the fact that he came after a lull in childbearing when she was a more mature twenty-eight help explain why she is investing in him in ways she had not had the luxury of doing with her older kids.

She now knows how to discipline without using a belt, and the value of grounding and time-outs. She spends her off time shuttling Christopher to and from school or to Little League practice in her new Chevrolet sport utility vehicle, an early benefit of her higher paychecks. When he has a science project, she's on the floor helping sculpt the volcano with him. She's quick to hug him and expects a kiss when she drops him off. She says he has become the very embodiment of the fresh start she was seeking for herself, and onto him she has grafted all her middle-class hopes.

He reminds her so much of Nicholas—the same round face and velvet skin, the same precociousness that she saw as impudence in young Nicholas when she was barely out of her teens, but now sees as reflecting her youngest's unlimited potential. While Nicholas went to a strapped public grade school in a perilous neighborhood, Christopher is in the gifted program of a school she handpicked on the middle-class side of town. While Nicholas played a hand-me-down Nintendo on a television with a busted tube, Christopher plays 3-D chess on the family's Dell computer.

Christopher is now ten, the same age as Nicholas when he appeared in the *Times*, but he talks like one of the sweet, smart-alecky kids on a network sitcom rather than a streetwise man-child who's seen too much too soon.

Asked what it means to be in the gifted program, he had a ready answer. "It means I'm smarter than the other kids," he said without flinching. At that age, Nicholas's conversations were about running from bullets.

DEMANDS AND RESPONSIBILITIES

At first, nursing was like hitting the lottery. She was making enough for the family to move into a four-bedroom apartment in a prewar building overlooking Lake Michigan. It has crown molding, a marble fireplace, and grander rooms than they have furniture for. She had a contractor paint the rooms the colors of sweet peas and corn on the cob. She bought a mahogany king-size bed, propping it high with pillows for herself and her husband, and bunk beds for the kids.

But she has found herself alone. She is making more money than anybody she knows. And come payday, everybody needs something, and not just the kids. Relatives need gas money, friends could use help with the rent. Even her patients, on hard times themselves, have their hands out.

"You got some money to lend me?" one of them, an older woman whose telephone had just been cut off, asked her. "You get your check yet?"

Suddenly, she is the successful star in her universe who is supposed to cover the cost of the family reunion, give career advice to the nieces and nephews, show up for their basketball games, float a loan to whoever needs it. After all, she's making $83,000 a year.

She is making more than her police detective husband and has found herself tiptoeing around his ego and expectations. They have tried different ways of dividing the bills, at one point splitting the $1,475 rent and sharing the utilities, at another point, one paying the rent and the other the utilities. But after Medicare and Social Security deductions and her share of the household obligations, groceries for a family of seven, her $500 monthly car payment, the assorted expenses that come with three teenagers, loans to relatives who think she makes a fortune, and the debt left over from her previous life, she finds that there is often little left over at month's end, and most months she's still in the hole.

She exists in an in-between place, middle class on paper but squeezed in reality. Take her car, for instance. It's a 2002 two-door Blazer that cost $29,000. She really needed the bigger four-door, just so everybody could easily get in. But that would have cost an extra $5,000, so everybody crams into the two-door. Insufficient though it is, it still comes at a high price. She pays 17 percent interest on the car loan—with $13,000 remaining—because of bad credit from her previous life, when sometimes the choice was whether to eat or pay the light bill.

The kids asked her the other day if she was getting a new car. "No," she said, "you can pop the seat and duck your head and get in like everybody else."

But she winces every time Christopher and Zach have to fold themselves into the size of a bag of groceries to fit into the rear storage compartment. She says she wants a bigger car like a Lincoln Navigator, but with gas so high she shudders at what it would cost to fill the tank, and she knows she can't afford a new car anyway.

So despite her income, Saks and Macy's are somebody else's world. Instead, she frequents the places she did in her previous life. She still shops at the dollar stores in Englewood, her old down-and-out neighborhood. On a recent trip to Louisiana for her family reunion she watched every nickel and checked her balance at the automated teller machine several times a day.

She has become keenly aware that what middle-class comforts she does enjoy are built on uncertain scaffolding. First, her status requires two paychecks and the stability and backup she gets from being married. It requires that she work the higher-paying twelve-hour night shifts that keep her away from her family for long stretches and leave her tired and irritable when she's with them.

It requires that her husband work extra hours as security at an elementary school, which leaves the two of them with little overlapping time to reinforce the strong marriage they need to stay where they are.

STRETCHING EVERY DOLLAR

Her job and paycheck say she's middle class, but what does that mean? She said that when she was on the outside looking in, she never imagined it would mean working three and a half years without a vacation or having an empty dining room waiting for a table and chairs. It never would have occurred to her that she would be working this hard and still have to choose between paying the phone bill and paying for her daughter Ishtar's prom.

She exhibits a mounting awareness of just how far her money will and will not go, and of how much hard work each dollar represents and how carefully she must protect it because any loss means she has to work that much harder.

So she drops what she's doing when she sees a spot on the sofa because it cost four figures and it's not paid for yet. She buys in bulk and has to watch out for relatives wanting to shop in her kitchen.

"I caught my aunt going into my pantry getting her some soap," she said. "I told her, 'That's Dove!'"

For Whitiker, being middle class has meant working upside-down hours for so long that she's started to greet people on the street with "Have a good evening!" It means taking on family members as unofficial patients with their edema and diabetes. "When you're the only nurse in the family they think you're a doctor," she says. "Mama calls me. Mama has her friends calling me."

She has no choice but to keep up the pace because she wants to get vested in the retirement plan at the hospital. She has eighteen months to go. She wants to open up a Roth retirement account, but can't seem to save enough. She wants to go back to school to get a bachelor's degree, but has neither the time nor the money.

"I feel like every corner of my body is being stretched," she said.

More than anything, Whitiker wants to buy a house. Sometimes she drives by her dream house on Greenwood in the comfortably middle-class neighborhood of Chatham. It's yellow brick with a spiral staircase and a two-story foyer and vertical blinds. But she's having trouble saving anything toward that house or any other. The bad credit from her previous life still haunts her. Where she wants to live, they can't afford. And where they could afford, she doesn't dare live.

"I have to live in a decent neighborhood," she said. "I can't walk around the projects in my nursing uniform. They would try to take everything I got. And my husband—he's arrested half the people in Englewood. We're in danger."

MISSING PIECES

Whitiker's ideal of middle-class perfection, with well-educated, smartly groomed kids gathered around a big middle-class dining room table, has two missing pieces: Nicholas and Willie. Her success came too late to benefit them. They were already on a road she was unable to steer them from. Nicholas dropped out of school in the eleventh grade and has been on and off the streets ever since. Willie, ever the follower looking up to Nicholas, was right behind.

At twenty-two, Nicholas is a burdened soul who saw too much too soon. His front tooth is broken from a fight he got into trying to protect Willie on the streets. His car has bullet holes from a drive-by shooting. He knows what it's like to have a pistol jammed into your chin, or to be a twelve-year-old making fifty dollars from neighborhood drug dealers for sitting on a hydrant and calling out "Five-O!"—street slang for the police. And worse.

"I could be dead right now," said Nicholas, his chiseled features weary, water welling in his eyes. "I should be dead. I hurt so many people. I hurt myself."

There were times when Allen, on patrol and by then Nicholas's putative stepfather, would catch him on the street and write up a summons but then let him go. But Nicholas finally got caught and spent about six weeks in jail in 2002 for stealing two coats from a Marshall's store in the suburbs and for fighting the police when they tried to arrest him, a consequence, his mother believes, of unresolved "anger issues" from the chaos of his childhood. She wishes she could go back and do some things differently. She thinks he needs to get into anger management and get into school to put his quick mind to good use.

For now, he lives in a walk-up apartment in the suburbs with the mother of the second of his three children; she's a housekeeper at the local YMCA. He has worked part-time as a stock clerk, but he is pinning his hopes on his rap music, which his exasperated mother admits is pretty good. He closes his eyes with hands quivering and begins one of his songs: "Going to change my ways," he sings in a near whisper. "Lord have mercy on me."

Willie has become a sturdily built young man with a movie star smile and a precisely trimmed goatee. Like Nicholas, he has worked low-paying service jobs when he has worked. He has two children, and a more serious criminal record that includes a felony drug conviction for selling near a school yard. "I was doing some things I shouldn't have been doing," Willie said, still sweet-faced at twenty-one.

Whitiker's two older sons are living reminders of the world she wants to put behind her. She lives in constant fear of what may happen to them.

"I go to work," she said wearily, "and I don't know when I'm going to get that call, that your son is dead or in jail again."

It was soon after she began working as a nurse that she got the call she had been dreading. She was in the intensive care unit bandaging a patient when she was called to the phone. Willie had been shot. It was not clear where he had been shot or how seriously hurt he was, or if he was conscious or would live.

She dropped everything. It turned out he had been shot twice in the leg. She found it suspicious that he was shot on a well-known South Side drug corner that had been contested by rival dealers. But she rushed in to save her son.

"It almost killed me," she said. "I almost had a nervous breakdown. I'm at work bandaging up patients, and I get the call that he's been shot. He said he was robbed. So I took him in and took care of his wounds."

In the summer of 2004, she got another call. She was at home in bed this time.

"Your son Willie's been shot," said the slurred, panicked voice on the phone.

It was a call from one of Willie's acquaintances from the very corner where Willie had been shot the first time.

"They were so ghetto," Whitiker recalled with exasperation. "They were arguing over the phone about what they should do."

She thought quickly. The nurse in her kicked into gear.

"Where was he shot?" she asked.

"In the leg," came the answer.

"Is he breathing?"

"Yeah."

She knew then that he would live.

"So I hung up and turned over and went to sleep," she recalled later. "I didn't even tell my family."

In the days and weeks that followed Willie's shooting, Whitiker made perhaps the most painful decision a mother could make in order to keep her family on the straight and narrow. She has performed a kind of emergency triage, banishing the infected to save the well.

She didn't visit Willie in the hospital, didn't take him home to tend him as she had the first time. She made it clear that neither he nor Nicholas was welcome until they got themselves together, got their high school equivalency diplomas, and started taking care of their kids. She has big plans for the younger ones: graduations, proms, college, professions. She doesn't want them getting shot like Willie.

"I told him you can't bring that here," she said. "How are his brothers supposed to feel? They're trying to do right and their brother is in the other room with a gunshot wound. I don't want him bringing that to the house and spreading it to the others. The other boys are on the right path, and I want it to stay that way."

Her plan appears to be working. The younger children rarely speak of Nicholas and Willie. When Willie showed up at the apartment one afternoon, Ishtar knew to alert her mother on her cellphone.

"Willie's here," Ishtar said. "What you want me to do?"

Everyone knows about the quarantine, even if it's breached. When Nicholas's name comes up, there's an awkward silence and a looking away.

PUSHING HIGHER GOALS

One Thursday in June 2005 was a big day for the family. It was the day Ishtar walked across the stage and became the first of Angela Whitiker's children to get a high school diploma. It caused quite a flurry in a family with a history of more births than graduations. After the ceremony, Whitiker's sister, Michelle, took Ishtar's yellow mortarboard and said, good-naturedly: "Let me try this on. Which way does it go? They don't give you these when you get your GED."

Everyone was there, except Willie, who was looking for work in Milwaukee, and Nicholas, who was in the public library reading up on contracts and music royalties to get a record deal. The day put Whitiker in a class quandary even as she went without a telephone to pay for the commencement and the prom.

While proud of Ishtar, who made it to the prom after all, Whitiker is torn between making a big deal of graduation and keeping it in perspective. "I'm not going to do like these other mothers and brag about, 'My baby graduated from high school!'" she said the other day. "I'm not going to say that's good. No, that's just the beginning. I want her to go to college and have a profession. She asked me, 'What age do you think I should have sex?' I said, 'I think about thirty.'"

Whitiker has made no attempt to hide her displeasure over Ishtar's wanting to join the navy—not only because her daughter could be deployed to the Middle East but also because it does not fit the middle-class ideal Whitiker now has for her children. She sees Ishtar going into law.

She is nudging fourteen-year-old John, who brings home As, is a linebacker on the football squad and a squad leader in the Reserve Officers Training Corps, to consider becoming a doctor. John listens and applies himself but says he wants to go into the army first. Before she became a nurse, the military might have been seen as a step up for her kids. Now she sees it as a detour from what they really should be doing.

"I try to talk to my kids to go into a profession," she said. "If you're certified and licensed, nobody can take that away from you."

To Nicholas and Willie, her advice is very different. "Can't you see your life is going down the drain, and you're the only one who can save it?" she asks to shrugging shoulders. "You want a quick way out. There is no quick way out. I tried that. It doesn't work."

But she still has hope. "I'm a late bloomer," she says, "and I know it's not too late for them."

REAL RICHES

What has kept Whitiker going is the knowledge that there are certain things no one can ever take away, that certain pieces of paper really do matter. That is why the letter she was afraid to open, the one announcing she had passed her nursing boards—it's folded up, crinkled in her wallet beneath a picture of her husband and her ATM card. The college diploma that it took her eight years to earn—her husband keeps that in his bedroom drawer, as if it is as much his as hers.

But as their second anniversary approached, the balancing act that plays out every day of their lives came down to the more immediate questions of getting by. Will they have a telephone this week or will Ishtar go to the prom? Will Whitiker be able to cut back her hours at the hospital and spend more time with her family? Can she work days instead of nights? Will she be able to find a home she can afford instead of spending five figures in rent each year?

Recently, she took a second job as a visiting nurse, checking in on elderly patients on the South Side during the day. It allows her to have more control over her schedule and work fewer nights at the hospital. The earnings potential is uncertain, and she has no health benefits under this new part-time arrangement, relying instead on her husband's. But a burden has been lifted for now.

So here she is on a late spring afternoon in her SUV running errands in the old neighborhood. She has always felt safest with the familiar. She drops off some clothes at the dry cleaner's where her sister's former husband's sister works. She buys a duffel bag at a dollar store that hired her aunt to fill in. She checks in on the niece who just had the caesarean. "How's the baby?" she asks. "You know I want to come up and give her some sugar."

Her cellphone rings.

"That's the kids," she said. She answers immediately, confident that, whatever bills are waiting in the mailbox, she's rich in the one thing that matters.

"Family is like the most important thing in life," Whitiker said. "Without family, I don't even see a purpose."

A Success Story That's Hard to Duplicate

The case of a welfare mother of six pulling herself into the ranks of the middle class is rare enough to compel experts on class and poverty to zero in on a single question: What would it take to create more Angela Whitikers?

"It shows the importance of work and marriage," said Sara S. McLanahan, a professor of sociology and public affairs at Princeton who specializes in family and poverty. "She found a good man and a good job. The thinking now is, it takes both to move out of poverty."

Walter Allen, a professor of sociology at the University of California, Los Angeles, whose areas of specialization include stratification and inequality, said: "She reflects a Horatio Alger kind of American dream story. The great news is that her efforts and initiative were rewarded. She got herself credentialed. The bad news is how challenging and how difficult it is to replicate her path."

The reason is that upward mobility requires what sociologists describe as the twin pillars of success: human capital and social capital. Human capital is a person's education, job credentials, and employability. Social capital usually means emotional support and encouragement from a reliable stakeholder in one's life, an asset commonly associated with marriage that is itself a form of wealth.

Often, single mothers have neither, as was the case with Whitiker. In fact, as a mother with six children by five fathers—a situation sociologists call multiple partner fertility—she faced more obstacles than most.

"The things going against this woman were phenomenal," McLanahan said. "Women who have children with other men are the least likely to find a mate."

In the current political climate, conservatives extol marriage as the solution to many of society's ills, while liberals argue that it alone cannot compensate for the effects of imperiled neighborhoods and failing schools. In fact, the research suggests that marriage may indeed be crucial to mobility out of poverty, but that it is not always enough.

Of the small number of poor single mothers who marry, 56 percent are lifted out of poverty, according to a 2002 study conducted by Signe-Mary McKernan and Caroline Ratcliffe for the Urban Institute. Getting a job is more common, and 39 percent of poor people who are hired rise out of poverty, as against 35 percent who get at least a two-year college degree.

Because of high rates of joblessness and incarceration among black men, marriage is not a viable option for many poor single mothers. Only 1.4 percent of them marry in any given year, the Urban Institute study found.

"Why do we feel that promoting marriage will solve the problem when there are so few marriageable men?" asked William Julius Wilson, professor of sociology and social policy at Harvard. "We need to find ways to duplicate the kinds of support that come from an encouraging partner."

Wilson says the government should increase its support for low-income women who want to go to college. "The more education these women receive, the more money they will make," he said. "They will be in different social settings and be exposed to more marriageable men."

"The liberals and the conservatives are both right in a sense," McLanahan said. "A good relationship is part of the story. But it can't be any relationship. It can't be any man. This case underscores that it must be a healthy relationship. The liberals are wrong because they're too dismissive of marriage, even though they want it for themselves. Everyone wants a strong helping hand. This woman represents the best of both ideals."

Still, the ups and downs of Whitiker's middle-class existence show that the transition out of poverty is not an easy one. "As well off as her economic situation is, her success is precarious," Walter Allen said. "This is a reminder that you can be middle class but in a very unstable situation."

For most of the country's history, race was a fairly clear class marker—black usually meant poor, and white middle class or better. Only in the second half of the twentieth century, with the dismantling of legal barriers to opportunity, did the lines begin to blur. Still, race continues to shape the experience of being middle class, sociologists say.

First, blacks tend to be first-generation middle class, as in Whitiker's case, which means they have fewer resources to draw upon as they navigate the middle-class world.

Second, there is the issue of wealth. "Not only do blacks earn less on average than whites, but the differences in wealth and race are staggering," Allen said. "Their status depends on current earnings, not accumulated wealth that provides a safety net. They don't come from families that could save and acquire property or teach them how things work in society, the mores and cultural capital.

"These things have not been as available to blacks as to whites. It translates into whether your family could buy that $23,000 home decades ago that is now worth $2 million or $3 million. Blacks weren't allowed to buy those $23,000 homes. Blacks fall at least a rung below their white counterparts because of the wealth factor alone."

There are other pressures as well, Wilson said. "Whites with the same educational attainment have better schooling and are able to get better jobs," he said. "Blacks are much more likely to live near poor segregated areas. They are much less insulated from crime and other manifestations of social disarray that grow from racial exclusion."

In the end, everyone profits when people like Angela Whitiker succeed, the experts said. "She is an object lesson," Allen said. "If you want to see this kind of success, you have to provide opportunity for a highly motivated woman to recover from her past mistakes. Ultimately, society benefits. Her younger children won't be a burden on society. And the next generation will do even better."

Encounters with Class

My Nanny Was a Dreadful Snob
Christopher Buckley

The first time I became aware of class? Darling, what a question, but here goes: my nanny was a dreadful snob.

I loved her dearly, but she was Canadian, born in the late nineteenth century, and thus deeply imbued with British class-consciousness. She read magazines that discussed in theological tones what Viscountess Margaret of Dimquith wore to tea with the Duchess of Wrenphrew—that sort of thing. (Today she would be reading *Hello*.)

I had two best buddies in those days. One lived down the street on his own private island connected by a causeway to the Connecticut mainland. His mother was John D. Rockefeller Sr.'s granddaughter. His father was a dear but somewhat purposeless fellow with the nickname of Bingo who seemed happiest shaking cocktails behind the bar. He called his wife Muffin. You would recognize them as Thurston and Lovey.

My other best buddy—who coincidentally had the same first name, but let's call him Tommy—lived on the other side of the woods in a pleasant working-class neighborhood made possible by the GI Bill. This Tommy's dad was a jovial, beer-bellied veteran of Iwo Jima who sold Mack trucks. He called his wife Marge. She called him Dick. You would recognize them as Homer and Marge.

When Tommy number 1 came over to play, bringing with him very cool toys (real guns, swords, tractors), my nanny would practically curtsey. "Can I get you a chocolate milk? How are your parents? I read that your older sister will be having her coming-out at the Colony Club this fall. How thrilling for her!"

When Tommy number 2 came over, also with cool toys (cherry bombs, copies of the latest *Playboy*), she would make no effort to conceal her disdain. "Oh, it's you, Tommy. Christopher can't play long today. He has to practice his piano and do his French lessons."

One day, after she had been particularly rude, I asked her why she didn't like Tommy 2. The papery skin of her aged brow furrowed and her eyes wandered about the room thoughtfully. I sensed that she was weighing her words, knowing that her answer would register on my young mind. Finally she threw up a hand and uttered a helpless "Oh, I don't know—he's so common."

A furious argument ensued touching on the theme of the Rights of Man and the Noble Savage, but there was no convincing her, and I was sent to bed with no TV that night.

I later related the incident to my mother, also Canadian-born and bred. She loved both Tommys equally. She smiled and said, "Well, you know, servants are the worst snobs of all." This put the matter in perspective for me. But I must confess that it wasn't until much later on that I realized that conversational mentions of "PLO" referred to the Palestine Liberation Organization, not to "People Like Ourselves."

Christopher Buckley is editor of Forbes FYI *magazine; his newest novel is* Florence of Arabia, *a Middle East comedy.*

Downwardly Mobile in Birmingham
DIANE McWHORTER

The part of Birmingham, Alabama, I grew up in was so class-conscious that a boyfriend broke up with me in ninth grade because my telephone exchange was not the socially obligatory 871 or 879. My lapse in standing was the misfortune of being from the *nouveau pauvre* side of what passed for an elegant family there in the Pittsburgh of the South.

Here is the visual image: My father, a downwardly mobile rogue, is putting in his annual appearance at the Mountain Brook Club, the snootiest of Birmingham's highly competitive country clubs, where his parents (Harvard Law, Wellesley) were charter members. As a club regular myself, I claw the rocks of terminal shame at these family gatherings, especially in the 1970s, when Papa shows up wearing a brown double-knit suit with tan top-stitching. But suave comrades from his suburban youth come by to shake hands, as if he had never left their silver midst. Joe, the colossal bartender, leaves his post to stare into my father's grinning face and clamp him in a bear hug. That is the most shocking greeting of all, because Birmingham is also known as the Johannesburg of America, the national bastion of apartheid. And one of the markers of my father's class rebellion is that he is so "outspoken" against members of Joe's race that he actually uses the N-word, which is verboten among polite southerners except when they are out of earshot of the children.

This scene is the perfect representation of how incoherent yet pervasive class is in America, built on a rickety foundation and decorated with trompe l'oeils that deceive us into thinking that we all do live in one big mansion. Social mobility is real, and goes in both directions, but no one loses track. And there is one class whose indifferent exclusivity remains perpetual: white.

Diane McWhorter is the author of Carry Me Home: Birmingham, Alabama: The Climactic Battle of the Civil Rights Revolution, *and a young adult history of the civil rights movement,* A Dream of Freedom.

From the Bronx to Cornell

RICHARD PRICE

A young transplanted Kentuckian living in an impoverished pocket of Cincinnati among families of similar background once said to me, "I never knew I was urban-Appalachian till I read it in a magazine."

In my experience, people who reside within socioeconomic shtetl-tags like "slum," "ghetto," "housing project," "inner city," or even "blue collar" mainly don't think of themselves as living in that particular cubbyhole; they see themselves as living in the world, since most everybody they associate with also calls that corner of it home, and chronically cash-strapped people tend not to travel all that much.

In most cases people have to physically leave the village, turn around, and look back to see where they came from before they can recognize not only its borders, both visible and invisible, but its very existence. For me, that started to come about in the fall of 1967, when I left Parkside Houses in the Bronx for college, or as someone's grandmother once called it, "sleepaway school."

Upstate, in Ithaca, my world was instantaneously turned on its head when I found myself lugging a suitcase along a cinderblock dorm corridor flanked by rooms that were populated by aliens from Boca Raton, Manhattan, Hong Kong, Short Hills, Guam, Marblehead, Barranquilla, and Murfreesboro.

In the ensuing culture-shocked days and weeks, it wasn't, for me, so much that the world began dividing itself into the haves and the have-nots as it was that I began to understand that the world was, in fact, the WORLD. That is to say, it was not just a compound of two dozen city-owned high-rises surrounded by asphalt-shingled or Formstone two-family houses. Class awareness, if you could call it that, seemed to fall more along the lines of aesthetics and experience than any bald expression of affluence. It seemed to me that everyone else's clothing was subdued and tossed together, not shiny, skintight, and painstakingly color-coordinated. Rumpled, apparently, was a look, not a sin. Small, well-handling

European cars were the ones to covet, not two-toned destroyer-length Cadillacs. Bob Dylan, despite his voice and appearance, was to be taken seriously, perhaps even more seriously than Frankie Valli. Smoking half a joint wasn't necessarily a one-way ticket to the booby hatch, and a den, I was gently told, was not the same as a basement.

One of the stranger effects of my fascination and hyperawareness of our differences was to semiconsciously cultivate an exoticness about myself, probably as an ego-survival countermeasure against what I perceived as the genuine exoticness of everybody else. So I developed a heavy Bronx accent up in Ithaca that I had never had at home. (I wasn't the only one: there was a kid from Mississippi who, by mid-October, had begun twanging and drawling to put the Snopes to shame, even though his father was both a poet and the headmaster of a boarding school down there.)

And in a continuation of the reverse whammy, I also began spinning tales about my (truly pedestrian) upbringing, some apocryphal, some with just a little narrative topspin to tidy up the endings. I became very good at it: in fact, a little too good. Two new friends whom I had invited to my home over the Thanksgiving break both canceled at the last minute. Later, back at school, they confessed to me that they had simply been too scared.

Three years after graduation, I was still at it, having published my first novel, *The Wanderers*, a collection of linked stories about a gang of Bronx teenagers in the pre-Beatles sixties. Both an author and a grad student at Columbia now, I affected an outerborough inflection at readings and in interviews that had become thick enough to require subtitles. And so it went for years, until the night it all came to an abrupt, mortified halt. In the summer of 1977, after a lecture and a long Q & A in a Midtown Manhattan bookstore, I was approached by a middle-aged man with an accent much like my own.

"You went to Cornell, right?"

"Yeah, I guess."

"That's amazing," he said, me trying not to grin. "Because my daughter? She goes to Bronx Community College, and she speaks better freakin' English than you."

Richard Price is the author of seven novels, including The Wanderers, Clockers, *and, most recently,* Samaritan.

At the Top of the Bottom in the Segregated South
DAVID LEVERING LEWIS

I think that I came to an appreciation of the concept of social class in my earliest years. The segregated South where I was born twenty-odd years before *Brown v. Board of Education* was a place of stark contrasts in black and white. "Negro" families of relative position and privilege, as mine was, inculcated the values of education, citizenship, and, as one said back then, breeding with a pertinacity that was as anxious as it was authentic. The rough, undiscerning democracy among prepubescent males was leavened by a narcissism of small differences of speech, color, dress, ambitions, etc., none too subtly imparted by watchful mothers whose silent prayer was, "There but for the grace of God . . ."

Both parents were educators, my father the principal of our city's first public high school for Negroes. We were people of consequence in the eyes of both "races," a family who lived, therefore, under the discipline of a double mandate: to be pillars, straitlaced and self-conscious, of social uplift in the community of color; and to serve, at best, as ameliorating agents of relations between the races and, at worst, as hired professionals of the Jim Crow order.

We lived well, our days were mostly sunny, and I know that my parents were stoically undeceived by the objectively equivocal, contingent nature of the advantaged life they gave me and my siblings. We knew we would go to college (with a detour for my older brothers in the segregated armed forces during World War II) and then become lawyers, doctors, teachers, and preachers. Within our cocoon of modest material possessions my playmates of the "right sort" and I envisaged a grown-up future of unexceptional assimilatedness. But the life of a class at the top of the bottom can be, and more often than not is, subject to irony, paradox, and the crisis of compromise. It was because of an all-of-the-above class lesson that I was spared a coming-of-age experience in the ex-Confederacy that I've never had great cause to regret. Because of my father's position, he had to take a position. He characteristically decided to stand on principle in a major civil rights case. He testified as an authority for the NAACP and against the discriminatory policies of the city public school system. The NAACP prevailed.

In less than a year, as I remember it, our family went from the top of the social heap to pariah status in the dominant community and to an awkward presence as unemployables among its own racial group. From this profoundly instructive trauma, I learned to assume the permanent possibility that, however solid the middle-class reinforcements, race could trump class in my life experience. But there is progress, I think. A broad national consensus now exists that, whenever it is socially and politically advantageous to do so, class considerations should trump racial identity. Race remains integral to Americans' perception of class, nevertheless. To deny its powerful, subsisting reality would be to endorse a simplistic and ultimately unhelpful evasion.

David Levering Lewis is a history professor at New York University and the author of a two-volume biography of W. E. B. DuBois, each volume of which won a Pulitzer Prize.

We Were Poor, but I Didn't Know It

Linda Chavez

Growing up in the mid-1950s and early 1960s in Denver, I had little sense of class differences. My classmates in parochial school in the center of town near the cathedral came from widely scattered neighborhoods: the middle-class area of two-story brick bungalows east of Cheseman Park; the Five-Points neighborhood near downtown, home to much of Denver's small black population; the Westside, where most Mexican-Americans lived; and North Denver, an area heavily represented by working-class Italian-Americans. Since we all wore uniforms—plaid jumpers for the girls and navy blue slacks and white shirts for the boys—it was difficult to know who was rich and who was poor.

Most children rode the city bus to school or walked, as I did the dozen or so blocks from where I lived, in a two-room basement apartment. The building had once been one of Denver's many mansions, built after the Gold Rush of the late 1800s. By the time we lived there, it had been broken into a warren of small apartments created from the many parlors and sitting rooms, with their pilasters, mahogany mantels, and stained-glass windows looking oddly out of place against the tattered furniture then occupying the space.

I had no sense that we were poor or struggling, even though my father had to stop working as a housepainter during Denver's long, cold winters. We shared a bathroom on the first floor of the apartment house with two other families. It was my job to post the sign-up list for bathing hours each week, so that no family monopolized the bathroom. Inevitably, the hot water ran out if you didn't take your bath early in the evening. Today, because this is America and you are not destined to remain in the class into which you were born, I live in a house with four bathrooms, and there is always enough hot water.

Linda Chavez is the president of the Center for Equal Opportunity, a syndicated newspaper columnist, and the host of a daily radio show, The Linda Chavez Program.

Appendix

The New York Times Poll on Class

The New York Times Poll that follows is based on telephone interviews conducted March 9 to 14, 2005, with 1,764 adults throughout
the United States. Interviews were conducted in English or Spanish.

The sample of telephone exchanges called was randomly se-
lected by a computer from a complete list of more than 42,000 active
residential exchanges across the country. Within each exchange, random digits were added to form a complete telephone number, thus
permitting access to listed and unlisted numbers alike. Within each
household, one adult was designated by a random procedure to be
the respondent for the survey.

For purposes of analysis, people with low household income or
high household income were oversampled, then weighted to their
proper proportion of the overall sample.

The results have also been weighted to take account of household size and number of telephone lines into the residence and to
adjust for variation in the sample relating to geographic region, sex,
race, Hispanic origin, marital status, age, and education.

In theory, in 19 cases out of 20, overall results based on such
samples will differ by no more than three percentage points in either direction from what would have been obtained by seeking out
all American adults.

For smaller subgroups the margin of sampling error is larger.
For example, it is plus or minus 4 points for low-income people and
7 points for high-income people.

In addition to sampling error, the practical difficulties of conducting any survey of public opinion may introduce other sources of error into the poll. Variation in the wording and order of questions, for example, may lead to somewhat different results.

Trends are based on nationwide *New York Times*/CBS News polls unless otherwise noted.

1. In order to make up for past discrimination, do you favor or oppose programs that make special efforts to help minorities get ahead? *THE ORDERING OF QUESTIONS 1 AND 2 WERE ROTATED*

	Favor	Oppose	DK/NA
12/6–9/97	55	39	7
2/6–10/00 CBS	59	32	9
6/21–27/00	50	39	11
7/13–17/00	53	38	9
1/19–22/03	53	39	8
7/13–27/03	53	40	7
3/9–14/05	**59**	**30**	**11**

2. Do you favor or oppose programs that make special efforts to help people get ahead who come from low-income backgrounds, regardless of their gender or ethnicity? *THE ORDERING OF QUESTIONS 1 AND 2 WERE ROTATED*

	Favor	Oppose	DK/NA
3/9–14/05	**84**	**10**	**6**

3. Currently the federal government taxes the assets—that is, the property and money—someone leaves when they die if the assets are worth more than a certain amount of money. Do you favor or oppose placing this tax on assets when someone dies?

	Favor	Oppose	DK/NA
3/9–14/05	**17**	**76**	**7**

4. If oppose, ask: What if the tax was only collected on estates worth more than $1.5 million? Then would you favor or oppose placing this tax on assets when someone dies?

	Favor	Oppose	DK/NA
3/9–14/05	27	46	3

5. Under the current law, the federal tax on estates will be phased out between now and 2010, when there will be no tax on estates at all. Unless Congress acts, the tax cut will then expire and the tax will again be collected on estates worth more than $1 million. Which comes closest to your opinion: 1. The federal government should tax estates worth more than $1 million; or 2. It should only tax estates worth more than $3.5 million; or 3. The federal tax on all inheritances should be permanently eliminated?

	More than $1M	More than $3.5M	Eliminate all estate tax	DK/NA
3/9–14/05	23	20	50	7

6. Do you think the justice system in the United States mainly favors the rich, mainly favors the poor, or does the justice system treat all Americans as equally as possible?

	Favor the rich	Favor the poor	Treats all equally	DK/NA
3/9–14/05	65	2	27	6

7. Do you think it's still possible to start out poor in this country, work hard, and become rich?

	Possible	Not possible	DK/NA
1/16–19/83	57	38	5
2/22–24/96	70	27	3
3/20–21/96 CBS	78	18	4
4/15–20/98 NYT	70	29	2

2/6–10/00 CBS	84	13	3
7/13–27/03	70	27	3
3/9–14/05	**80**	**19**	**2**

8. In your opinion, in America, how much tension is there between poor people and rich people—a lot, some, not much, none at all, or depends?

	A lot	Some	Not much	None at all	Depends	DK/NA
3/9–14/05	**34**	**44**	**14**	**3**	**1**	**4**

9. In general, do you feel that organized labor has too much power in the United States, not enough power, or is it about right?

	Too much power	Not enough power	About right	DK/NA
3/9–14/05	**32**	**21**	**40**	**7**

Varied wording: In general, do you feel that organized labor has too much power in the United States, or does not have too much power in the United States? *Time* magazine poll conducted by Yankelovich, Skelly & White, Nov. 5–7, 1985: 50%—Has too much power; 38%—Does not have too much power; 12%—Not sure.

10. In general, do you feel that Americans who are very rich have too much power in the United States, not enough power, or is it about right?

	Too much power	Not enough power	About right	DK/NA
3/9–14/05	**72**	**1**	**23**	**4**

Varied wording: In general, do you feel that Americans who are very rich have too much power in the United States, or do not have too much power in the United States? *Time* magazine poll conducted by Yankelovich, Skelly & White, Nov. 5–7, 1985: 68%—Have too much power; 23%—Do not have too much power; 8%—Not sure.

11. Do you think you will reach, as you define it, the "American dream" in your lifetime, or have you already reached it?

	Already reached it	Will reach it in lifetime	Will not reach it in lifetime	DK/NA
8/13–16/92	37	43	17	4
12/1–3/95	45	35	16	5
3/9–14/05	**32**	**38**	**27**	**3**

12. What does the phrase "American dream" mean to you?

	3/9–14/05
Financial security/steady job	**19**
Freedom/opportunity	**20**
Have a house/home	**13**
Family	**7**
Happiness/contentment/peace of mind	**19**
"Life in America"	**1**
Good job	**1**
Successful	**7**
Health	**2**
Comfortable retirement	**2**
To pay little/no taxes	**—**
Doesn't exist/illusion/nothing	**2**
Other	**2**
DK/NA	**5**

13. Compared to your parents when they were the age you are now, do you think your own standard of living now is much better, somewhat better, about the same, somewhat worse, or much worse than theirs was?

	Much better	Somewhat better	About the same	Somewhat worse	Much worse	DK/NA
1/27–5/31/94*	31	32	21	11	3	2
2/1–5/25/96*	32	29	21	12	4	2
2/1–6/19/98*	33	31	21	10	3	2
2/1–6/25/00*	34	31	21	9	3	2
2/6–6/26/02*	33	33	19	11	3	1
3/9–14/05	**39**	**27**	**20**	**9**	**4**	**1**

*General Social Survey conducted in-person by the National Opinion Research Center of the University of Chicago.

14. Do you have any children? If yes, ask: Are any of your children under eighteen?

	Yes, under 18	Yes, over 18	No	DK/NA
3/9–14/05	**39**	**24**	**37**	—

15. *If parent:* When your children are the age you are now, do you think their standard of living will be much better, somewhat better, about the same, somewhat worse, or much worse than yours is now?

	Much better	Somewhat better	About the same	Somewhat worse	Much worse	DK/NA
1/27–5/31/94*	18	32	23	17	5	5
2/1–5/25/96*	22	30	21	18	5	4
2/1–6/19/98*	24	36	22	10	4	5
2/1–6/25/00*	32	34	18	8	3	4
2/6–6/26/02*	29	38	20	9	2	2
3/9–14/05*	**25**	**31**	**18**	**15**	**7**	**5**

*General Social Survey conducted in-person by the National Opinion Research Center of the University of Chicago.

16. Looking ahead, how likely is it that you will ever be financially wealthy? Would you say it is very likely, somewhat likely, not very likely, or not at all likely?

	Very likely	Somewhat likely	Not very likely	Not at all likely	Already rich	Depends	DK/ NA
3/9–14/05	**11**	**34**	**30**	**22**	**1**	**1**	**1**

17. We talk a lot about people being in one or another social class—the middle class, or the working class, or the upper class. We'd like to know what these terms mean to people nowadays. What do you think determines what social class a person is in?

	3/9–14/05
Income	**24**
Education	**7**
Occupation/job	**6**
Values/Behavior	**4**
Possessions	**1**
Social standing	**2**
Environment	**1**
Background/Religion	**2**
Wealth/money/net worth	**38**
Nothing	**—**
Other	**2**
DK/NA	**14**

18. We have some questions about opportunities for getting ahead. How important do you think coming from a wealthy family is for getting ahead in life—essential, very important, somewhat important, not very important, or not important at all?

	Essential	Very important	Somewhat important	Not very important	Not at all	DK/NA
1987*	4	19	28	30	17	3
2000*	3	16	27	33	14	8
3/9–14/05	**11**	**33**	**40**	**10**	**6**	**1**

*General Social Survey conducted in-person by the National Opinion Research Center of the University of Chicago. Question read: "To begin, we have some questions about opportunities for getting ahead. . . . Please show for each of these how important you think it is for getting ahead in life. First, how important is coming from a wealthy family? Essential, very important, fairly important, not very important, not important at all."

19. How important do you think having a good education is for getting ahead in life—essential, very important, somewhat important, not very important, or not at all important?

	Essential	Very important	Somewhat important	Not very important	Not at all	DK/NA
1987*	35	49	13	1	—	1
3/9-14/05	**39**	**46**	**12**	**2**	**—**	**—**

*General Social Survey conducted in-person by the National Opinion Research Center of the University of Chicago. Question read: "To begin, we have some questions about opportunities for getting ahead. . . . Please show for each of these how important you think it is for getting ahead in life. . . . Having a good education yourself? Essential, very important, fairly important, not very important, not important at all."

20. How important do you think natural ability is for getting ahead in life—essential, very important, somewhat important, not very important, or not at all important?

	Essential	Very important	Somewhat important	Not very important	Not at all	DK/NA
1987*	13	47	33	3	—	2
3/9-14/05	**22**	**49**	**26**	**1**	**—**	**2**

*General Social Survey conducted in-person by the National Opinion Research Center of the University of Chicago. Question read: "To begin, we have some questions about opportunities for getting ahead. . . . Please show for each of these how important you think it is for getting ahead in life . . . Natural ability?—how important is that? Essential, very important, fairly important, not very important, not important at all."

21. How important do you think hard work is for getting ahead in life—essential, very important, somewhat important, not very important, or not at all important?

	Essential	Very important	Somewhat important	Not very important	Not at all	DK/NA
1987*	36	52	9	1	—	1
3/9–14/05	**46**	**41**	**11**	**2**	**—**	**—**

*General Social Survey conducted in-person by the National Opinion Research Center of the University of Chicago. Question read: "To begin, we have some questions about opportunities for getting ahead. . . . Please show for each of these how important you think it is for getting ahead in life . . . Hard work—how important is that for getting ahead in life? Essential, very important, fairly important, not very important, not important at all."

22. How important do you think knowing the right people is for getting ahead in life—essential, very important, somewhat important, not very important, or not at all important?

	Essential	Very important	Somewhat important	Not very important	Not at all	DK/NA
1987*	9	35	42	11	2	2
3/9–14/05	**16**	**33**	**42**	**6**	**2**	**—**

*General Social Survey conducted in-person by the National Opinion Research Center of the University of Chicago. Question read: "To begin, we have some questions about opportunities for getting ahead. . . . Please show for each of these how important you think it is for getting ahead in life . . . Knowing the right people? Essential, very important, fairly important, not very important, not important at all."

23. When you think about your current financial situation, what, if anything, worries you the most?

	3/9–12/95	**3/9–14/05**
Don't have enough money	19	**21**
Losing job/job stability	17	**11**
Health care	7	**11**
Retirement	6	**8**
Economy getting worse	6	**6**
General fear about the future	5	**3**
Social Security	4	**4**
Paying for children's college	4	**6**
Paying credit card/loan debt	4	**4**

Taxes	3	**3**
Interest rates	2	—
National deficit/debt	2	**1**
Nothing	12	**12**
Other	2	**3**
DK/NA	7	**6**

24. A person's social class is determined by a number of things, including education, income, occupation, and wealth. If you were asked to use one of these five names for your social class, which would you say you belong in—upper class, upper middle class, middle class, working class, or lower class?

	Upper	Upper Middle	Middle	Working	Lower	DK/NA
3/9–14/05	**1**	**15**	**42**	**35**	**7**	**1**

25. Which social class was your family in when you were growing up—upper class, upper middle class, middle class, working class, or lower class?

	Upper	Upper Middle	Middle	Working	Lower	DK/NA
3/9–14/05	**1**	**8**	**28**	**44**	**18**	—

26. Are you now married, widowed, divorced, separated, or have you never been married?

	Married	Widowed	Divorced	Separated	Never married	DK/NA
3/9–14/05	**57**	**7**	**10**	**2**	**24**	—

27. If married: What social class was your (husband's/wife's) family when he/she was growing up—upper class, upper middle class, middle class, working class, or lower class?

	Upper	Upper Middle	Middle	Working	Lower	DK/NA
3/9–14/05	1	8	31	43	15	2

28. Would you say MOST members of your extended family—that is, the members of your family who you do not live with—are in the same social class as you are, or not?

	Yes	No	DK/NA
3/9–14/05	66	32	2

29. If yes, ask: Would you say most members of your extended family are in a higher social class or a lower social class?

	Higher	Lower	DK/NA
3/9–14/05	16	14	2

30. If married: At the time you got married, what was the last grade in school you had completed?

	Not a H.S. grad	H.S. grad college	Some grad	College	Postgrad	Refused
3/9–14/05	11	33	28	22	6	—

31. If married: And when you got married, what was the last grade in school your (husband/wife) had completed?

	Not a H.S. grad	H.S. grad college	Some grad	College	Postgrad	Refused
3/9–14/05	9	37	22	22	8	2

32. What one thing do you think of as a symbol of wealth and status in the United States?

	3/9–14/05
Money/bank account	22
Freedom/opportunity	2

Have a house/home	**26**
Family	**1**
Happiness/contentment/peace of mind	**1**
"Life in America"	**1**
High-paying job/successful career	**5**
Successful	**1**
Health	**1**
Comfortable retirement	**—**
Power	**3**
Second home/vacation home	**1**
Vehicles	**4**
Celebrity	**1**
Specific items (Rolex, Super Bowl tickets)	**1**
Consumer goods, in general	**1**
Own business	**1**
Education	**2**
Location/address	**2**
Charity/generosity/doing for others	**—**
Other	**5**
DK/NA	**21**

33. Compared to thirty years ago, do you think the likelihood of moving UP from one social class to another is greater today, less today, or is it about the same?

	Greater	Less	Same	DK/NA
3/9–14/05	**40**	**23**	**35**	**2**

34. Compard to thirty years ago, do you think the likelihood of moving DOWN from one social class to another is greater today, less today, or is it about the same?

	Greater	Less	Same	DK/NA
3/9–14/05	**39**	**17**	**41**	**3**

35. Compared to European countries, do you think it is easier in the United States to move up from one social class to another, harder, or about the same?

	Easier	Harder	Same	DK/NA
3/9–14/05	46	13	26	16

36. Have you ever moved because of a job? If yes, ASK: How often have you moved because of a job?

	No, never	Once	Twice	Three times	Four or more times	DK/NA
3/9–14/05	65	14	9	4	8	—

37. If married: Have you ever moved because of your (husband's/wife's) job? If yes, ASK: How often have you moved because of (his/her) job?

	No, never	Once	Twice	Three times	Four or more times	DK/NA
3/9–14/05	77	12	4	2	4	—

38. How important to you is being involved in your community—very important, somewhat important, not very important, or not at all important?

	Very important	Somewhat important	Not very important	Not at all important	DK/NA
7/17–19/99 NYT	35	51	14	1	
3/9–14/05	44	45	8	3	—

39. How important to you is your being physically attractive—very important, somewhat important, not very important, or not at all important?

	Very important	Somewhat important	Not very important	Not at all important	DK/NA
7/17–19/99 NYT	18	55	21	6	—
3/9–14/05	**16**	**54**	**19**	**9**	**1**

40. How important to you is having faith in God—very important, somewhat important, not very important, or not at all important?

	Very important	Somewhat important	Not very important	Not at all important	DK/NA
7/17–19/99 NYT	75	17	8	4	1
3/9–14/05	**74**	**16**	**5**	**4**	**1**

41. Do you feel you have enough time for yourself, or not?

	Yes	No	DK/NA
6/20–25/89	62	38	1
3/9–14/05	**58**	**41**	**1**

42. Do you feel you spend too much time, not enough time, or about the right amount of time with your family?

	Too much	Not enough	Right amount	DK/NA
6/20–27/89*	5	47	46	3
9/1991*	6	36	56	2
3/9–14/05	**3**	**40**	**56**	**1**

*Mellman & Lazarus poll for Mass Mutual.

43. About how much money per year do you think the typical American family of four needs to make in order to be considered rich?

	Under $100,000	$100,000–$199,999	$200,000–$299,999	$300,000–$399,999	$400,000–$499,999
3/9–14/05	**16**	**29**	**19**	**5**	**3**

	$500,000–$749,999	$750,000–$999,999	$1 million	Over $1 million	DK/NA
3/9–14/05	**6**	**2**	**5**	**3**	**14**

44. To help a child make the most of his or her life, how important do you think physical activities and sports are—essential, very important, somewhat important, not very important, or not important at all?

	Essential	Very important	Somewhat important	Not very important	Not at all important	Depends	DK/ NA
3/9–14/05	25	42	28	4	1	—	1

45. To help a child make the most of his or her life, how important do you think special tutoring for college preparation is—essential, very important, somewhat important, not very important, or not important at all?

	Essential	Very important	Somewhat important	Not very important	Not at all important	Depends	DK/ NA
3/9–14/05	15	36	35	8	3	3	1

46. Do you think Americans are feeling more social pressure these days to buy luxury items like bigger homes and expensive cars in order to keep up with other people, or not?

	More pressure	No more pressure	DK/NA
3/9–14/05	81	16	3

47. What do you think is the yearly household income for the average family of four in the United States?

	Under $30,000	$30,000– $39,999	$40,000– $49,999	$50,000– $59,999	$60,000– $69,999
3/9–14/05	6	15	20	17	12

	$70,000– $79,999	$80,000 or more	DK/NA
3/9–14/05	7	8	14

48. To get ahead in life, how much formal education do you think a person needs—a high school diploma, some college education, a four-year college degree, or does a person need to get a postgraduate degree?

	H.S. grad	Some college	College grad	Postgrad	Don't need H.S. diploma	DK/NA
3/9–14/05	7	20	51	17	2	3

49. Do you think most people who enlist in the U.S. military these days are from low-income families, middle-income families, or high-income families?

	Low	Middle	High	Low & Middle	DK/NA
3/9–14/05	51	37	1	8	4

50. Do you think the social and economic background of the people in the U.S. military accurately reflects the makeup of the United States, or not?

	Yes	No	DK/NA
3/9–14/05	39	52	9

51. In recent years, have you ever taken on more debt than you should have in order to pay for items like a bigger home or expensive car or other types of luxuries? If yes, ask: What did you buy?

	3/9–14/05
No	76
House	6
Second home	—
Cars	11
Specific items	1
Consumer goods, in general	2
Vacation	1

Special event (wedding, graduation)	—
Children's education	—
Other	1
DK/NA	1

52. Do you personally feel a strong connection with your neighbors and the neighborhood where you NOW live, some connection, or no connection, at all?

	Strong connection	Some connection	No connection at all	DK/NA
3/9–14/05	31	51	18	—

53. Would you say you have been able to put down roots in your community, or have you found it difficult to become part of the community where you now live?

	Roots	Difficulty in becoming part	DK/NA
4/6–9/91*	83	16	1
3/9–14/05	75	21	4

*Los Angeles Times poll

54. Do you ever feel as if you're at risk of falling out of your current social class?

	Yes	No	DK/NA
3/9–14/05	18	81	1

55. How concerned are you that in the next twelve months you or someone else in your household might be out of work and looking for a job—very concerned, somewhat concerned, or not concerned at all?

	Very	Somewhat	Not at all	DK/NA
3/31–4/2/96	37	25	37	2
9/2–4/96	21	26	51	2

10/3–5/02	31	20	48	1
4/23–27/04	33	25	41	1
6/23–27/04	28	27	45	—
9/12–16/04	30	26	44	—
10/14–17/04	22	24	53	1
3/9–14/05	**22**	**25**	**53**	—

56. How worried are you about not having enough money for retirement—very worried, somewhat worried, or not at all worried? (BASED ON RESPONDENTS WHO ARE NOT RETIRED)

	Very	Somewhat	Not at all	DK/NA
12/3–6/95 NYT	35	42	22	—
3/5–14/05 NYT	34	41	25	—
3/9–14/05	**34**	**48**	**18**	**1**

57. Do you rent your home, or are you buying it with a mortgage, or is it entirely paid for?

	Rent	Mortgage	Paid for	DK/NA
3/9–14/05	**28**	**45**	**25**	**2**

58. On a scale of one to ten, where one is extremely poor and ten is extremely rich, where would you place your family's financial situation now compared with all other American families?

	One	Two	Three	Four	Five	Six	Seven	Eight	Nine	Ten	DK/NA	Mean
3/9–14/05	2	2	9	16	33	17	14	4	1	—	2	5.2

59. Using the same one-to-ten scale, again one is extremely poor and ten is extremely rich, where do you expect your family's financial situation to be in ten years?

	One	Two	Three	Four	Five	Six	Seven	Eight	Nine	Ten	DK/NA	Mean
3/9–14/05	1	1	4	7	21	17	22	16	3	2	6	6.2

60. What was the last grade in school your mother completed?

	Not a H.S. grad	H.S. grad	Some college	College grad	Postgrad	DK/NA
3/9–14/05	26	37	12	12	3	10

61. What was the last grade in school your father completed?

	Not a H.S. grad	H.S. grad	Some college	College grad	Postgrad	DK/NA
3/9–14/05	29	32	10	11	7	12

62. Are you currently employed, or are you temporarily out of work, or are you not in the market for work at all? If not in the market for work: Are you currently retired or not?

	Currently employed	Out of work	Not in market	Retired	DK/NA
3/9–14/05	59	9	11	20	—

63. *If employed:* How satisfied are you with your job—very satisfied, somewhat satisfied, somewhat dissatisfied, or very dissatisfied?

	Very satisfied	Somewhat satisfied	Somewhat dissatisfied	Very dissatisfied	DK/NA
12/3–6/95 NYT	43	42	11	4	
12/8–11/96 NYT	45	40	9	6	—
7/17–19/99 NYT	47	41	8	4	
3/9–14/05	47	41	9	4	—

64. What is your occupation? If necessary: What exactly do you do for a living? What is your job title? If retired, ask: What was your occupation?

	3/9–14/05
Executive/High-Level Management	2
Professional/Other Managers/Artists	19
Technical/Administrative	19
Clerical	7
Skilled Labor	15
Unskilled Labor	5
Service Workers/Protective Services	26
Housemaker	1
Student	1
Other	1
DK/NA	3

65. *If married:* Is your (husband/wife) currently employed, or is (he/she) temporarily out of work, or is (he/she) not in the market for work at all? If not in the market for work: Is your (husband/wife) currently retired or not?

	Currently employed	Out of work	Not in market	Retired	DK/NA
3/9–14/05	65	6	9	20	—

66. *If spouse is employed:* What is your (husband's/wife's) occupation? If necessary: What exactly does he/she do for a living? What is his/her job title? If retired, ask: What was (his/her) occupation?

	3/9–14/05
Executive/High-Level Management	2
Professional/Other Managers/Artists	20
Technical/Administrative	21
Clerical	9
Skilled Labor	14
Unskilled Labor	6
Service Workers/Protective Services	20

Homemaker	**2**
Other	**1**
DK/NA	**3**

These last few questions are for background only. Some people are registered to vote and others are not.

67. Are you registered to vote in the precinct or election district where you now live, or aren't you?

	Yes	No	DK/NA
3/9–14/05	**80**	**20**	**—**

68 *If registered:* Did you vote in the 2004 presidential election, did something prevent you from voting, or did you choose not to vote? If voted, ASK: Did you vote for John Kerry, George W. Bush, or Ralph Nader?

	Kerry	Bush	Nader	Voted, won't say for whom	Didn't vote	DK/NA
3/9–14/05	**42**	**42**	**—**	**5**	**10**	**2**

69. Generally speaking, do you usually consider yourself a Republican, a Democrat, an Independent, or what?

	Republican	Democrat	Independent	DK/NA
3/9–14/05	**31**	**35**	**29**	**6**

70. How would you describe your views on most political matters? Generally do you think of yourself as liberal, moderate, or conservative?

	Liberal	Moderate	Conservative	DK/NA
3/9–14/05	**22**	**36**	**37**	**5**

71. Would you describe your health as excellent, good, only fair, or poor?

	Excellent	Good	Only fair	Poor	DK/NA
3/9–14/05	30	51	15	4	—

72. Do you live in an apartment or a house?

	Apartment	House	DK/NA
3/9–14/05	19	80	—

73. Do you ever buy lottery tickets?

	Yes	No	DK/NA
3/9–14/05	42	57	—

74. Some people think of themselves as evangelical or born-again Christians. Do you ever think of yourself in either of these ways?

	Yes	No	DK/NA
3/9–14/05	29	69	2

75. Would you say you attend religious services every week, almost every week, once or twice a month, a few times a year, or never?

	Every week	Almost every week	Once/ twice a month	A few times a year	Never	DK/ NA
3/9–14/05	29	10	13	28	19	1

76. How important is religion in your daily life? Is it extremely important, very important, somewhat important, or not at all important?

	Extremely important	Very important	Somewhat important	Not at all important	DK/ NA
3/9–14/05	28	33	25	12	1

77. Have you yourself ever served in the U.S. armed forces or the U.S. reserves?

	Yes	No	DK/NA
3/9–14/05	15	85	—

78. Do you or does any member of your immediate family now serve in the armed forces or in the U.S. reserves?

	No	Yes, self	Yes, other	Yes, self and other	DK/NA
3/9–14/05	83	2	15	—	—

79. What is your religious preference today?

	Protestant	Catholic	Jewish	Muslim	Other	None	DK/NA
3/9–14/05	53	24	2	1	7	11	3

80. How old are you? Are you between 18 and 29, 30 and 44, 45 and 64, or are you over 64?

	18–29	30–44	45–64	Over 64	Refused
3/9–14/05	22	29	32	16	1

81. What was the last grade in school you completed?

	Not a H.S. grad	H.S. grad	Some college	College grad	Postgrad	Refused
3/9–14/05	11	32	29	18	10	1

82. If married: What was the last grade in school your (husband/wife) completed?

	Not a H.S. grad	H.S. grad	Some college	College grad	Postgrad	Refused
3/9–14/05	8	33	22	21	14	2

83. Are you of Hispanic origin or descent, or not?

	Hispanic	Not Hispanic	Interviewed in Spanish	DK/NA
3/9–14/05	8	87	4	1

84. Are you white, black, Asian, or some other race?

	White	Black	Asian	Other	Refused
3/9–14/05	78	12	1	8	1

85. Was your total family income in 2004 under or over $50,000? If under $50,000: Was it under $15,000, between $15,000 and $30,000, or was it between $30,000 and $50,000? If over $50,000: Was it between $50,000 and $75,000, between $75,000 and $100,000, or was it over $100,000? If over $100,000: Was it over $150,000, or not?

	Under $15,000	$15,000– $29,999	$30,000– $49,999	$50,000– $74,999
3/9–14/05	10	19	20	21

	$75,000– $100,000	$100,000– $150,000	Over $150,000	Refused
3/9–14/05	12	7	4	6

86. How many members of your household currently contribute to your family's total annual income?

	One	Two	Three	Four or more	DK/NA
3/9–14/05	41	50	3	2	3

87. Gender

	Male	Female
3/9–14/05	48	52

Internet Resources

The complete "Class Matters" newspaper series, including audioclips, photographs, and interactive graphics, is available at http://www.nytimes.com/class.